CW01483775

teach
yourself

**business french
culture book**

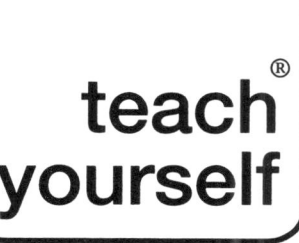

business french
culture book
sarah carroll
emmanuel lainé

For over 60 years, more than
50 million people have learnt over
750 subjects the **teach yourself**
way, with impressive results.

be where you want to be
with **teach yourself**

For UK order enquiries: please contact Bookpoint Ltd, 130 Milton Park, Abingdon, Oxon, OX14 4SB. Telephone: +44 (0) 1235 827720. Fax: +44 (0) 1235 400454. Lines are open 09.00–17.00, Monday to Saturday, with a 24-hour message answering service. Details about our titles and how to order are available at www.teachyourself.co.uk.

For USA order enquiries: please contact McGraw-Hill Customer Services, PO Box 545, Blacklick, OH 43004-0545, USA. Telephone: 1-800-722-4726. Fax: 1-614-755-5645.

For Canada order enquiries: please contact McGraw-Hill Ryerson Ltd, 300 Water St, Whitby, Ontario L1N 9B6, Canada. Telephone: 905 430 5000. Fax: 905 430 5020.

Long renowned as the authoritative source for self-guided learning – with more than 50 million copies sold worldwide – the **teach yourself** series includes over 500 titles in the fields of languages, crafts, hobbies, business, computing and education.

British Library Cataloguing in Publication Data: a catalogue record for this title is available from the British Library.

Library of Congress Catalog Card Number: on file.

First published in UK 1999 by Hodder Education, 338 Euston Road, London, NW1 3BH.

First published in US 1999 by The McGraw-Hill Companies, Inc.

This edition published 2007.

The **teach yourself** name is a registered trade mark of Hodder Headline.

Copyright © 2007 Sarah Carroll Limited

Typeset by Transet Limited, Coventry, England.
Printed in Great Britain for Hodder Education, a division of Hodder Headline, an Hachette Livre UK Company, 338 Euston Road, London, NW1 3BH, by Cox & Wyman Ltd, Reading, Berkshire.

The publisher has used its best endeavours to ensure that the URLs for external websites referred to in this book are correct and active at the time of going to press. However, the publisher and the author have no responsibility for the websites and can make no guarantee that a site will remain live or that the content will remain relevant, decent or appropriate.

Hodder Headline's policy is to use papers that are natural, renewable and recyclable products and made from wood grown in sustainable forests. The logging and manufacturing processes are expected to conform to the environmental regulations of the country of origin.

Impression number   10 9 8 7 6 5 4 3 2 1
Year   2010 2009 2008 2007

contents

About the author

Sarah Carroll has lived in France and worked with French-speaking colleagues around the world. She has a BSc (Hons) degree in European Management Science (French) and spent a year at the University of Strasbourg under the first year of the European ERASMUS programme, which promotes mobility among students in Europe. She also has an MPhil from the University of Swansea, Wales, and holds the Trinity College Certificate qualifying her to teach French to adults.

Sarah spent ten years with global management consultancies Accenture and Deloitte Consulting, where she worked with and managed multicultural and multilingual teams. She found out by harsh experience that it is really worth paying attention to 'all this language and cultural stuff' if you want to make things happen.

Fuelled by her passion for languages and culture, she has founded two businesses. The first is Grow Global (**www.growglobal.biz**), a business consultancy which supports companies looking to become more international. Sarah is also registered by the British Chambers of Commerce to deliver Export Communications Reviews on behalf of UK Trade & Investment, helping companies to communicate as effectively as possible when exporting. The second business is Language Advantage (**www.languageadvantage.com**), an international website which provides language plans, language courses and many extra ways to really learn a language. Find out more at **www.sarahcarroll.com**

This book is dedicated to my grandmother, Dorothy Harris, who awakened my passion for all things French.

About the consultant

Emmanuel Lainé is from northern France and has been living in the UK since 1999. He has worked for many worldwide companies within international teams. Before that he studied for his French Diploma of Engineering in Compiègne, France, and also has an MSc in Advanced Materials from Cranfield University in the UK.

He then used his engineering expertise and worked for global leaders in optical telecommunications, Nortel Networks and Bookham, before moving to the financial sector in the City of London for two years with roles as a dealer and project manager. He has now moved back to where his heart is and is studying towards a PhD in Mechanical Engineering at Imperial College, sponsored by the international company Caterpillar.

Rarely, and in addition to his scientific mind, he is interested in any creative venture and finds every opportunity to express himself. He writes reviews for the website **www.language advantage.com** as well as exploring his passion for poetry by publishing on-line at **www.allpoetry.com**.

Acknowledgements

Thanks to each of you for helping us in a personal or professional way to get *Teach Yourself Business French* up and running: Joe Carroll, Susan Carroll, Helen Carter, Estelle Dingley, Sue Hart, Alex Jaton, Marie-Christine Lainé, Michel Lainé, Andrea Martins.

introduction

This *Teach Yourself Business French* culture book is a workbook – a self-help book, if you like. We want to help you to be where you want to be with teach yourself – and you want to be doing business in French-speaking countries. As well as learning the business language of France, you need to transform yourself into a perfect citizen of the world of French business. And that is where the self-help bit comes in.

You need two main things to get you on the right tracks: knowledge and skills. With these you can become a global business success, someone who can communicate successfully with colleagues, customers and business partners from anywhere in the French-speaking world. You will do much better in international business if you are aware of the culture – the general culture and the business culture – of your customers, colleagues and business partners.

The knowledge zone

The first part is about knowledge. You need to build new relationships. The bottom line is that you need to have something to talk about and you need to know what you're talking about to gain respect and trust. You'll get to know so much with our overview of the French language and the francophone world, because there is so much more to it than just France. With our snapshot of the main French-speaking economies where you're likely to be doing business, you'll never be short of something to say to your new clients or colleagues.

The business culture zone

The second part is about skills. You need to be able to play the part of a business person in your new culture. First, you'll need to think about how you 'are' when you're doing business. We'll give you an introduction to the fascinating subject of cultural awareness and intercultural management and you'll come out of this feeling a much more rounded, worldly-wise person. We'll give you some food for thought about whether you prefer to focus on the differences – or similiarities – between you and your French-speaking equals.

The French business zone

The third part starts homing in on the detail. You can take a closer look at some important elements of French culture and how they can impact on the French business culture and business environment. It's important to understand what makes a country and its people the way they are – so often the history, the structure, the geography and so many other 'basic' facts about a country influence both the development of that country and its people – and will most definitely have an impact on the way that business is carried out in that culture. You'll not only get pointers about what to do and what not to do, but you'll also find out why business is the way it is in France and French-speaking countries.

The reference zone

This final part tells you how to get hold of more information about the topics we have covered so that you can complete your research. A lot of it is available free on the internet, but you can also delve into our suggested reading list too. You need to become a walking encyclopedia about your target country.

Armed with these skills – and a global mindset – you'll soon be able to do business effectively in French-speaking countries. You will be prepared and confident.

We want this book to act as your personal coach for all things business French. So we've kept it short and included only the essentials (the bare minimum you should know). We've put information into tables where possible to give you 'at a glance' answers and save you even more time. But with this comes a warning: you may find that this book actually ends up sparking off as many new questions as it answers the original questions you had.

You should be able to read the culture book in a day. Start right now, as we know that just reading this book can improve the way you do business in French-speaking countries, which will improve your business relationships and ultimately increase your sales. What better reason do you need?

Enjoy our tour of the French-speaking business world and let us know of your experiences or questions at **businessfrench@hodder.co.uk**.

Sarah Carroll

knowledge zone

01

the francophone world

The French-speaking world
stretches across all
continents of the world.

Starting from its historical home in France, French extends its reach to its neighbours in Europe (Belgium, Luxembourg and Switzerland) and even has official language status in other adjoining countries such as Italy and Jersey, which is part of the United Kingdom. Also, nestled on the south coast of France facing the Mediterranean Sea, is the French-speaking Principality of Monaco.

The former French colonies stretch worldwide. In Africa, there are over 20 countries that have French as their official language alongside their national languages. They are clustered in West and Central Africa, but can also be found in Djibouti in the east as well as some island states off the south-eastern coast of the African mainland. Many of the now independent states have been influenced greatly by French administration during colonial days and still maintain strong cultural and economic links with France. The emergence of some of the stronger African economies onto the world stage over the coming decades could see an interesting change in the balance in the French-speaking world.

Over the Atlantic to the Americas, and large parts of Canada are French speaking, fanning out from Québec, the centre of the French-speaking world in Canada. A tiny French-speaking territory with a population of under 10,000 lies off the east coast of Canada and still remains part of France. A throwback to history means there are many people around New Orleans in the USA who speak French Creole and there are over 1.5 million French speakers in the whole of the USA. French has even extended its reach to the edge of the Caribbean and the Spanish-speaking enclave of South America where it is an official language in French Guiana as well as to the Pacific Ocean and Antarctica, where France still retains territories.

French does not belong to France.

Interview between Tirthankar Chanda, journalist, and Secretary General of the International Organisation of the Francophonie (IOL), Abdou Diouf.

Source: **www.diplomatie.gouv.fr**

Map 1: the French-speaking world

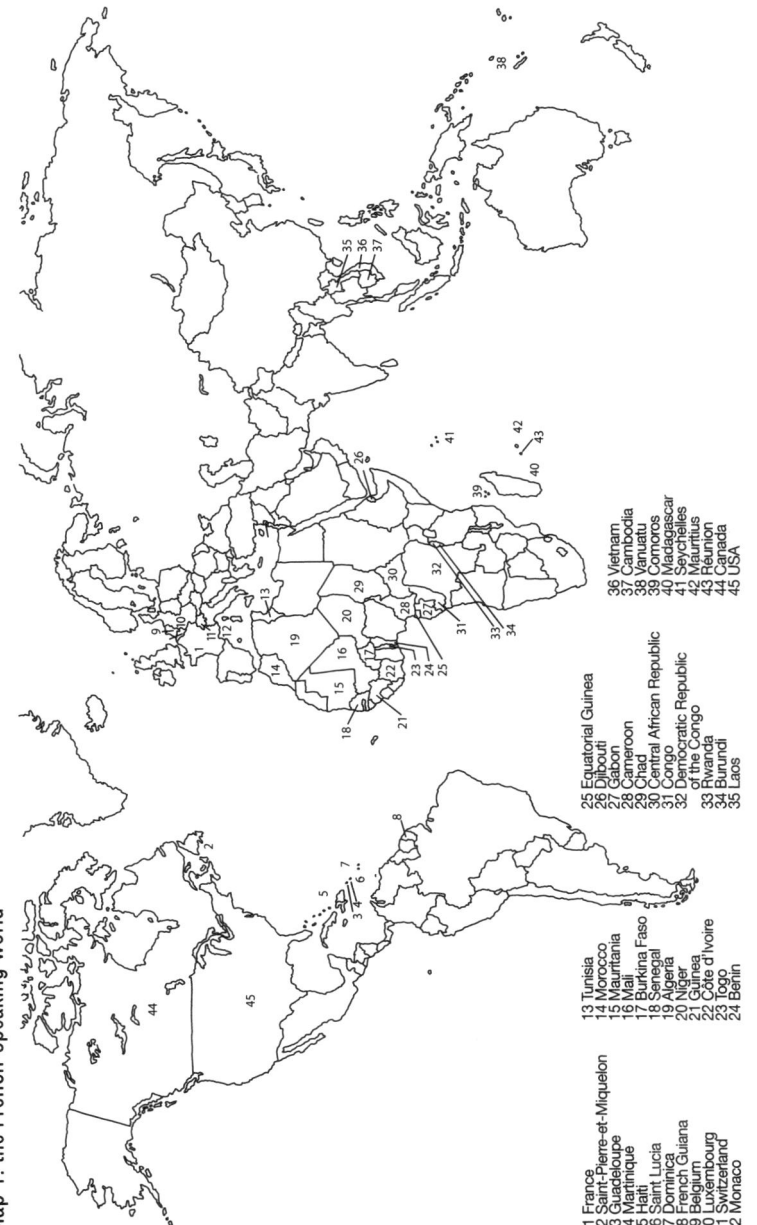

1 France
2 Saint-Pierre-et-Miquelon
3 Guadeloupe
4 Martinique
5 Haiti
6 Saint Lucia
7 Dominica
8 French Guiana
9 Belgium
10 Luxembourg
11 Switzerland
12 Monaco

13 Tunisia
14 Morocco
15 Mauritania
16 Mali
17 Burkina Faso
18 Senegal
19 Algeria
20 Niger
21 Guinea
22 Côte d'Ivoire
23 Togo
24 Benin

25 Equatorial Guinea
26 Djibouti
27 Gabon
28 Cameroon
29 Chad
30 Central African Republic
31 Congo
32 Democratic Republic
   of the Congo
33 Rwanda
34 Burundi
35 Laos

36 Vietnam
37 Cambodia
38 Vanuatu
39 Comoros
40 Madagascar
41 Seychelles
42 Mauritius
43 Reunion
44 Canada
45 USA

French is spoken to a different extent in over 50 countries in the world. For some it is a first language – the mother tongue – and for others it is a second or even a third language alongside other national or local languages.

In 32 countries, French is the official language and it is frequently woven into the fabric of the constitution. French may be spoken by the whole population (as in France) or by part of the population (as in Canada and in Switzerland).

In about a further 20 countries French is a national language, often used for education, government and diplomacy. French is often in widespread use either as a business language or as a 'common' language in countries where there are many local languages and dialects or where France had colonies throughout the centuries. French may be used as a spoken language, but not necessarily as a written language.

Some countries have been classed as francophone countries as they have large French-speaking populations and actively encourage French culture. These include countries such as Albania, Bulgaria, Czech Republic, Lithuania, Macedonia, Moldavia, Poland, Romania and Slovenia.

There are 1.6 million French-speakers in the USA, which is more than in Switzerland.

Base population data source: **www.census.gov**

Table 1: French-speaking countries and territories

Europe
Andorra*
Belgium
France
Italy
Luxembourg
Monaco
Switzerland
United Kingdom (Channel Islands)
Americas
Canada

Dominica*
French Guiana
Guadeloupe
Haiti
Saint Lucia*
Saint-Pierre-et-Miquelon
USA*
Asia
Cambodia*
Lao People's Democratic Republic*
Vietnam*
Australasia
French Polynesia
New Caledonia
Vanuatu
Wallis and Futuna
Antarctica
French Southern & Antarctic territories
Africa
Algeria*
Benin
Burkina Faso
Burundi
Cameroon
Central African Republic
Chad
Comoros Islands
Congo
Côte d'Ivoire
Democratic Republic of Congo
Djibouti
Egypt*
Equatorial Guinea
Gabon
Guinea
Lebanon*
Madagascar
Mali
Martinique
Mauritania*
Mauritius
Mayotte
Morocco*

Niger
Réunion
Rwanda
Senegal
Seychelles
Togo
Tunisia*

* indicates widely used only, all others official or national language

More information

www.academie-francaise.fr
www.census.gov
www.diplomatie.gouv.fr
www.francophonie.org
www.un.org

02

the French language

There are about 350 million French speakers in the world.

There are potentially 350 million French speakers in the world, including those speaking it as a first or second language. In comparison, there are nearly 1 billion Mandarin Chinese speakers, 500 million English speakers and 350 million Spanish speakers. French is ranked between the fifth and fifteenth most spoken language in the world, depending on who you ask and what you count. One thing is sure, though, alongside English, French is the only language spoken on every continent of the world.

The French-speaking world is still growing and with the rapid population growth predicted for many African countries, the population could reach 700 million by 2050. The popularity of the French language continues with over 80 million people learning French in the world and in 2006 it became the sixth most widely-used language on the web.

> **The French-speaking world is still growing and could reach over 700 million by 2050.**
>
> Base population data source: **www.un.org** population prospects 2006

The importance of French

The importance of French as a global language is related more to its spread across the world, than to the absolute number of speakers of French. French speakers, native and learners alike, are passionate and proud of the French language. More than anything, it acts as an important element of cultural identity for either their home, or adopted, nation.

French is still seen as a diplomatic language in international organizations and institutions, the best known being the European Union, the United Nations and the International Olympic Committee where it is one of the official languages. It is also the uniting language of the African Union. In much of Africa, French is seen as a route to a good education and, beyond that, to a more engaging and prosperous working life.

The spread of French speakers

The top 20 French-speaking countries give a potential French-speaking population – as a first or second language – of 325 million and include:

Table 2: top French-speaking countries by population in millions (2006)

1	France	63.4
2	Democratic Republic of the Congo	62.6
3	Madagascar	19.7
4	Côte d'Ivoire	19.3
5	Cameroon	18.5
6	Burkina Faso	14.8
7	Niger	14.2
8	Senegal	12.4
9	Mali	12.3
10	Chad	10.8
11	Belgium	10.5
12	Rwanda	9.7
13	Haiti	9.6
14	Guinea	9.4
15	Benin	9.0
16	Burundi	8.5
17	Switzerland	7.5
18	Togo	6.6
19	Central African Republic	4.3
20	Congo	3.8

Base population data source: **www.un.org** population prospects 2006 & **www.insee.fr** French population 2006

There are also nearly 9 million French speakers in Canada, with over 7 million in Québec and over 1 million in other provinces, such as Ontario, Manitoba and New Brunswick as a result of the early French colonies in eastern Canada.

Perhaps one of the most surprising concentrations of French speakers is in the USA, where there are about 1.6 million. This is more than the number of French speakers in Switzerland. French is the second most widely-spoken language in four states: Louisiana, Maine, New Hampshire and Vermont. Louisiana used to be a French colony from 1682 and was finally sold to the USA in 1803. From early colonization, French influence spread from the cities of Detroit, through St Louis to Baton Rouge and down to New Orleans.

The origins of the French language

For the linguistically-minded among you, French is a member of the family of Indo-European languages, and more specifically, the Italic and Romance languages. As such, it has 89 per cent of its language in common with Italian, 75 per cent with Portuguese, Romanian and Spanish, 29 per cent with German and 27 per cent with English.

The history of the French language

Most French grammar and vocabulary came from spoken Latin. It is thought that the earliest evidence of written French was in the ninth-century *Les Serments de Strasbourg*, alongside a German version.

In the Middle Ages, French varied greatly from region to region and there were many different dialects across France. The main distinction was between those speaking *la langue d'oïl* (in the north) and *la langue d'oc* (in the south). The *langue d'oïl* gradually took precedence and became known as Old French (*l'ancien français*).

In 1536, Latin ceased to be the administrative language of France. Middle French (*le moyen français)* emerged in the fourteenth and fifteenth centuries when it gradually lost the declension system and was replaced with the more traditional sentence structure of subject, verb and object. In the sixteenth century, French was imposed as an administrative language instead of Latin.

In the seventeenth and eighteenth centuries, Classical French (*le français classique)* became the language of the aristocracy across most of what is now northern and eastern Europe, including as far away as Poland. It also emerged as the diplomatic language of the world, with major treaties being prepared in French, when before they would have been written in Latin. The influence of the French language stretched beyond the bounds of the French Empire at the time.

The words *oïl* and *oc* both meant yes.

Source: **www.diplomatie.gouv.fr**

Variations of French

When doing business in French-speaking countries in Europe, you can expect to use 'global' French or 'standard' French. Generally, you should be able to understand the French spoken in a business environment.

You may find slightly different accents, pronunciation and vocabulary both within France and as you cross into bordering countries in Europe. The most marked difference between French in France is between that used in the north and south, which throws back to the days of the *oïl* and the *oc*.

In Canada, you are likely to hear more differences in the French used, including Americanisms, or adaptations thereof, in daily use in the spoken language.

On the African continent, you are more likely to see variations in the use of words and again differences in accents. Also, most people speak French alongside their local languages, so there will be seepage from those languages into French, in much the same way that you end up with *franglais*.

Dialects and local languages

There are many regional languages in France including: Alsacien, Basque, Breton, Catalan, Corsican and Flamand. There are many more in the French-speaking world, with some of the most well-known being: Walloon (Belgium), Picard (Belgium), Genevois (Switzerland), Québecois (Canada), Acadien (Canada), Jerriais (Jersey, UK) and Cajun French (USA).

Organizations promoting French

L'Académie française

In 1635, *l'Académie française*, based in Paris, was founded to create a common French language across all territories of France at that time. Today, it continues to regulate the French language and to counteract the infiltration of English and the import of anglo-americanisms. The Academy will create a French word if none exists, rather than adopting the English equivalent. This will also occur if a new idea or concept has been invented and needs to be named. Examples are: *courriel* rather than 'email' and *logiciel* instead of 'software'. In practice, as many people adhere to the 'rules' set out by the Academy as break them and you are very likely to hear the anglo-americanisms in use every day in the business world.

Members of *L'Académie française* are given seats and called *immortels*.

Source: **www.academie-francaise.fr**

L'Office québécois de la langue française (OQLF)

The original office was set up in 1961 before it became the Québec Office of the French Language. It was given a wider mandate in 1977 with the Charter of the French Language. A further bill was passed by the Québec National Assembly in 2003, and it is taken very seriously and has been allocated an annual budget in the region of $20 million. French is one of the offical languages of Canada alongside English and was made so through the Official Languages Act of 1969, which was revisited in 1988. This means that federal services have to be offered in both languages where the population size demands it.

Similar to *l'Académie française*, the *OQLF* works mainly to define terminology and to promote the use of French, 'so that French is the usual and normal language of work, communications, trade and businesses in the Administration and companies'. Although some English-speaking Canadians are sceptical and dimissive about the *OQLF*, it is enshrined in law and does have the power to impose fines.

Conseil Supérior de l'audiovisuel (CSA)

France's *CSA* has as a mission, under laws of 1986 and 1994, '*à la défense et à l'illustration de la langue française*', that is to ensure the correct use of French in audio and visual media. It works to maintain the quality of French in use on French radio, televisions and screens and also provides a list of French terminology that can be used as an alternative to English.

Institut Français/Alliance Française

These two organizations have centres around the world and encourage cultural exchanges, as well as promoting teaching and the use of the French language. It is a now a massive network present in 90 countries, which has taught over 80 million learners in 130 countries with nearly 1 million teachers.

More information

www.academie-francaise.fr
www.alliancefrancaise.org.uk
www.census.gov
www.csa.fr
www.diplomatie.gouv.fr
www.ethnologue.com
www.francophonie.org
www.insee.fr
www.institut-francais.org.uk
www.internetworldstats.com
www.oqlf.gouv.qc.ca
www.un.org

03

a snapshot of France

France has been one of the most politically and economically important countries in the world.

For many centuries, France has provided a strong cultural influence across the globe. You need to know why, so we have selected some of the most important facts and figures about France for you.

France at a glance

Official name	Republic of France
	République française
Borders	Andorra, Atlantic Ocean, Belgium, English Channel, Germany, Italy, Luxembourg, Mediterranean Sea, Monaco, Spain, Switzerland
Capital	Paris
Population	63.4 million
Official languages	French
Currency	Euro
Time zone	GMT +1
International phone code	+33
Domain extension	.fr
Main business centres	Bordeaux, Lyon, Marseille, Paris, Strasbourg, Toulouse
Top companies (2005)	Aventis, AXA, BNP Paribas, Carrefour, Crédit Agricole, Crédit Lyonnais, Peugeot, Renault, Société Générale, Total

Location

There is more to France than meets the eye. Apart from being one of the biggest and most dominant countries in Western Europe, its territories extend to all continents on Earth.

France itself is made up of mainland (often called *metropolitan*) France, which is divided into 26 regions, 22 on the mainland and four overseas. These regions are further divided into 96 departments. Two of France's main departments lie on the island of Corsica and there are also a number of overseas territories, which are collectively know as DOM-TOM (which stands for *départements d'outre-mer* and *territoires d'outre-mer*).

The four overseas departments (DOM) are: Guadeloupe and Martinique in the Caribbean, French Guiana (*la Guyane*) in South America and Réunion (off the east coast of Africa).

The overseas territories (TOM) include: French Polynesia (in the Pacific Ocean, off the coast of Australia), Wallis and Futuna (again off the Australian coast), Saint-Pierre-et-Miquelon (off the east coast of Canada) and the French Southern and Antarctic Territories in the Pacific (Kerguelen, Crozet, Saint Paul et Amsterdam, Terre Adélie). The territory of New Caledonia (*la Nouvelle-Calédonie*) in the Pacific Ocean is transferring some government duties under the 1998 *Accord de Nouméa*, pending a referendum on independence scheduled for between 2014 and 2019. Mayotte (off Madagascar in the Pacific Ocean) has been designated as a *collectivité départmentale* by France since 2001, pending full *département d'outre-mer* status.

Some of these territories became part of France as early as the sixteenth century as a result of French colonialism and many stayed as such until the 1960s. The first explorers set out from France in the early 1500s.

Geography

France is the largest country by area in Western Europe with a total area of 550,000 km^2. It is 1,000 km from north to south and also from east to west.

France is also known as *l'Hexagone* as its shape roughly looks like a hexagon. On two sides of the hexagon to the north-east and east are borders with Belgium, Germany, Luxembourg, Switzerland and Italy. Moving round to the south, it has the Mediterranean Sea and its borders with Monaco, before arriving in the south-west and its borders with Spain and Andorra. The other two sides of the hexagon and the rest of its borders are with the Atlantic Ocean in the west and with the English Channel in the north.

France has 5,500 km of coastline where its many rivers meet the sea, including the Seine, the Loire, the Rhône and the Saône, the Garonne and the Dordogne. It also has one of Europe's great rivers, the Rhine, on its north-eastern border.

Two-thirds of mainland France is plain, covered by farms (50 per cent) and forests (30 per cent). It also has some very mountainous regions with many substantial ranges such as the

Alps, Pyrenees, Jura, Vosges and the Ardennes on its borders, as well as the Massif Central, a former volcanic region, at its centre. France's highest mountain, Mont Blanc, is in the Alps and measures 4,808 metres.

There are three main climate zones in France: oceanic in the west, mediterranean in the south and continental in central and eastern regions.

Population

The population of mainland France is now over 63 million, making it one of the largest countries in the European Union. It has a very multicultural population due to its colonial past, its policy of encouraging immigration in the post-World War II era and its continued close ties with French-speaking Africa. Latest figures indicate that the French population is made up of over 5 million people of Arab and African descent. Nearly 5 per cent of the population is made up of people from other nationalities living in France, such as those emigrating from the UK and Germany.

The most populated cities in France are: Paris with a population of 2 million (11 million in the Île de France region), Marseille with 0.8 million (1.5 million in the Marseille–Aix-en-Provence region), Lyon with just under half a million in the city and 1.5 million in the region. After Lyon, the cities become much smaller.

Table 3: top French towns by population

1	Paris	2,154,000
2	Marseille	821,000
3	Lyon	466,000
4	Toulouse	435,000
5	Nice	348,000
6	Nantes	282,000
7	Strasbourg	273,000
8	Montpellier	244,000
9	Bordeaux	231,000
10	Lille	225,000

Source: **www.insee.fr** (population estimates 2005, rounded)

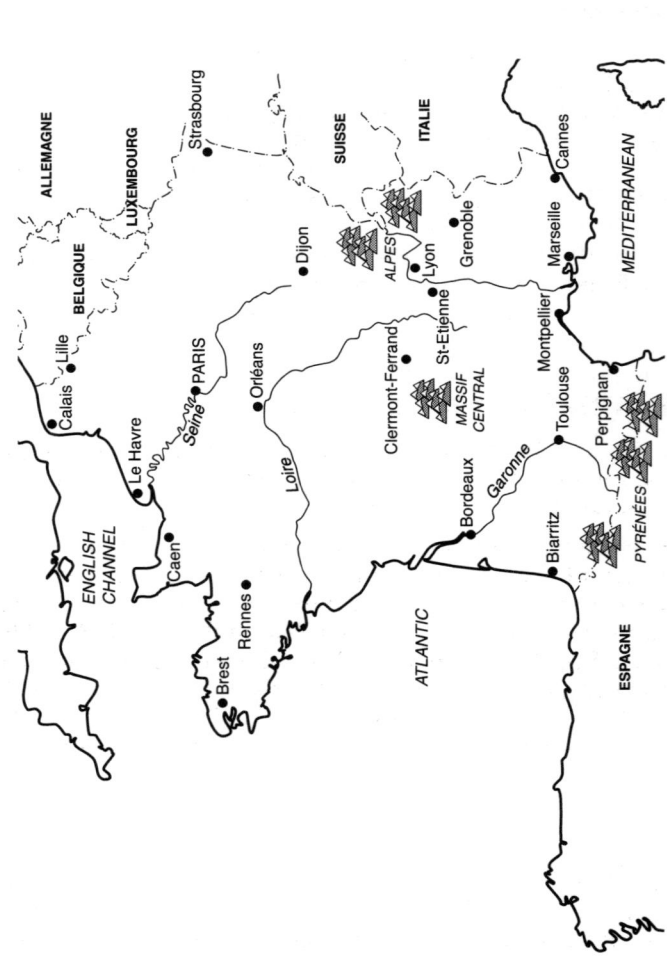

Map 2: France

Language

French is the official language of France and in 1992 a new line was added to the French Constitution stating that '*la langue de la République est le français*' ('the language of the Republic is French'). However, other languages, dialects and regional variations are spoken in France as well as many community languages.

Religion

France is a secular state and so all religions, faiths and beliefs can be found within the country. The traditional religion of France has been Catholicism and over two-thirds of people still claim to be Catholic. Stemming from immigration in the 1960s and 1970s from North Africa, France has one of the largest Muslim populations in Europe with up to 10 per cent of the population. Protestantism (2 per cent) and Judaism (1 per cent) are also represented and France has one of the largest Jewish populations in Europe. The remaining French report that they have no religious affiliation or do not disclose their religion.

National identity

The country became the Republic of France (*la République française*) in 1792 after the French Revolution. Paris has been the capital of France since 486.

The tricolour flag (blue, white, red) has been the official standard of the French Republic since 1789 when the colour white was added to the red and blue of the Paris National Guard to become the national flag. The motto of the French Republic is *Liberté, Egalité, Fraternité* ('Liberty, Equality, Fraternity'). The *Marseillaise* became the national anthem of France on 14 July 1795. It was composed in Strasbourg in 1792 by Rouget de Lisle and was originally known as the Battle Hymn of the Army of the Rhine.

History

France is as old as history itself and through time has helped shape western civilization as we know it today.

The land mass that is today's France is thought to have been formed about 500 million years ago. Much later, the mountain ranges of the Massif Central, Vosges and Ardennes were created. The sea flooded the region repeatedly between 180 million and 80 million years ago. The Pyrenees are thought to have been formed between 150 million and 40 million years ago and the Alps from between 65 million and 2 million years ago.

France has much evidence of ancient inhabitants, including the oldest human remains in Tautavel in the Pyrenees, which are believed to date back 450,000 years as well as the famous stones of Carnac in Brittany, which are believed to have been constructed between 5,000 BC and 2,000 BC.

France was plagued by invasions from 1,000 BC to Roman times, including invasions by Celts, Liguarians (from the south-east), Iberians (from the south-west) and Greeks (from the south). The Romans invaded in around 58 BC and made Lyon the capital. Many centuries of peace followed up until 400 AD. Yet more invasions from many fronts including the Vandals, Visigoths, Alamans, Franks and Huns changed the cultural mix yet again. The Vikings invaded still later in the late 800s.

Table 4: defining moments in French history

481–511	Clovis became the first King of Franks. His aim was to unite all Franks.
768–814	Charlemagne became King of Franks. He built the Empire of France (including Austria, Germany, Italy, Switzerland, Belgium, Luxembourg, Netherlands).
1066	The Normans invaded England.
1170	The University of Paris was founded and higher education begins.
1337–1453	The Hundred Years War took place involving Joan of Arc (*Jeanne d'Arc*).
1461–83	Louis XI consolidated France.
1500s and 1600s	The establishment of universities (Toulouse, Montpellier, Orléans).
1500s	The first explorers set off to colonize the Americas, Africa and Asia.

1598	Edict of Nantes gave the freedom of conscience to all.
1643–1715	Louis XIV (Sun King) imposed royal control and oversaw the removal of the Edict of Nantes.
14 July 1789	The French Revolution took place with the storming of the Bastille. This saw the end of the monarchy.
1789	The French constitution (*liberté, egalité, fraternité*) and *départements* were born.
1792–1804	The First Republic came into being with Napoléon Bonaparte as First Consul.
1804–14	This was the time of the First Republic with Napoléon Bonaparte as Emperor. During this period France enjoyed military glory, control of most of Western Europe and saw the introduction of the *Code Napoléon* and the legal system.
1814–48	This was the time of the Monarchists, which saw the Restoration and the July Monarchy. This period ended in revolution.
1827	The first French railway was built.
1848–52	This was the period of the Second Republic, which ended with a coup.
1850s	The time of the Industrial Revolution.
1852–70	These were the years of the Second Empire under Emperor Napoléon III. It was a time of social justice.
1870–1940	The period of the Third Republic.
1870–1	The Franco-Prussian War.
1889	The Eiffel Tower was built. It was the tallest building in the world until 1930.
1900	The first line of the *Métro* opened in Paris.
1905	Following the Dreyfus affair, the Church and State are separated by law.
1914–1918	World War I.

1939–45	World War II.
1946–54	The French Indochina War.
1954–62	The Algerian War of Independence.
1946–58	The period of the Fourth Republic.
1958	France became a founding member of the European Economic Community.
1958	The Fifth Republic starts with Charles de Gaulle as President.
May 1968	Student riots occur in Paris and across France.
1969	The first Concorde flight.
1979	The launch of the Ariane 1 rocket.
1981	The launch of the TGV train.

Structure

The constitution of the Fifth Republic came into force on 4 October 1958 and is occasionally amended to reflect fundamental changes to the needs of the country. It is overseen by the Constitutional Council, which has nine members.

The President of the Republic is elected for a five-year term. Nicolas Sarkozy is the current President and was elected for a first term in May 2007, making him the sixth President of the Fifth Republic. The next Presidential elections will take place in 2012. The previous Presidents of the Fifth Republic are: Jacques Chirac (1995–2007), François Mitterand (1981–95), Valéry Giscard d'Estaing (1974–81), Georges Pompidou (1969–74) and Charles de Gaulle (1959–69).

The President appoints the Prime Minister who then assembles the Government. The Prime Minister works with the government to set out and implement national policy and legislation under the watchful eye of Parliament. Parliament has two assemblies: the Senate comprising senators appointed for a six-year term with half the members renewed every three years and the National Assembly with deputies elected for a five-year term.

There are a large number of political parties in France which are ever changing. Currently, the main political parties fall into two groups, the left and the right. Some of the more popular political parties are :

- *Union pour un mouvement populaire (UMP)*
- *Parti socialiste (PS)*
- *Union pour la démocratie française (UDF)*
- *Front national (FN)*
- *les Verts*
- *Parti communiste français (PCF).*

The far right National Front (*Front national*) is very active and credible in France, and is led by Jean-Marie Le Pen, who was a Presidential candidate in 2007 and came fourth in the first round with over 10 per cent of the vote. His daughter is now active in the party.

There are also a number of political parties from the regions, with strong separatist movements:

- *Abertzaleen Batasuna* (from the Basque country)
- *Alsace d'abord* (from Alsace)
- *Ligue savoisienne* (from Savoie)
- *Union Démocratique Brettonne* (from Brittany)
- *Unione Naziunale (*Corsica).

Administratively speaking, metropolitan France (including Corsica) has 96 *départements* which are grouped into 22 *régions* and are divided into *arrondissements* (326). These are subdivided into *cantons* (3,827) and then *communes (36,538).* The regions are now taking on more of an administrative function.

Paris is famous for its *arrondissements* and has 20 of them. From an administration point of view, these are technically *cantons*.

Source: **www.diplomatie.gouv.fr**

Economy

France was an early trading nation and so has been one of the world's richest nations since the days of colonization in the seventeenth century and the Industrial Revolution in the nineteenth century. Today, it is one of the world's largest economic powers in terms of GDP with a high standard of living and a strong health, education and social security system.

About 75 per cent of people are employed in services, just over 20 per cent in industry and commerce, and nearly 4 per cent in agriculture. Important sectors include aerospace, transport, telecommunications, pharmaceuticals, banking, insurance, tourism, luxury products, research, high technology and car manufacturing. Another important sector is tourism. France is the most visited country in the world with over 75 million foreign tourists. France is one of the largest agricultural producers in the world and products include cereals, wine, livestock, diary, fruit and vegetables. This sector is undergoing major change as a result of reform of the European Union's Common Agricultural Policy (CAP) and various worldwide trading agreements.

France does not have many natural energy sources and has practically no oil, but provides a high percentage of its own energy requirements through the development of nuclear and hydroelectric power. Alternative sources of power such as solar and wind are becoming important and account for about 5 per cent of energy production.

The country joined the euro (€) on 1 January 1999, when it became the French official currency. It became the sole legal tender in the country in 2002. Although accepting the currency, the French population rejected a referendum on the new proposed EU constitution in 2005.

France's economy is greatly influenced by the global market, in particular by the USA and Germany. It is an active member in many of the international organizations, such as the European Union, G8, United Nations, NATO, World Trade Organisation and the OECD.

France is the world's fourth largest exporter of goods and the second largest exporter of services and agriculture. Its main export partners are Germany, Spain, Italy, UK, Belgium, Luxembourg, Spain and the USA. It does 65 per cent of its trade within the EU25 (2005 figures). Main exports include intermediate goods, capital goods, consumer goods, motor vehicles and processed food and drink. Its main import partners are Germany, Italy, Spain and the UK. Just over 60 per cent of its imports are from the EU25 (2005 figures). The main imports are intermediate goods, capital goods, consumer goods, motor vehicles and, importantly, energy.

Infrastructure

France has a very good rail system operated by the SNCF. It was one of the first countries in the world to introduce the high-speed train, the TGV (*le train à grande vitesse*). Trains can reach 270 kph (165 mph) on specially laid track. The rail system is also well linked to other parts of Europe through dedicated trains such as the Thalys (from Paris to Amsterdam) and the Eurostar (from Paris to London via the Channel Tunnel).

France has many large international airports including Paris Charles de Gaulle, Paris Orly, Bordeaux and Lyon. There is a good network of regional airports, many of which are served by low-cost airlines, contributing to France's status as one of the most visited countries in the world. The national airline is Air France.

France has one of the most dense road networks in Europe with many kilometres of toll motorway. Marseille is the largest port and France takes advantage of its long coastline with many other major ports operating both cargo and passenger services.

More information

www.assemblee-nat.fr
www.conseil-constitutionnel.fr
www.conseil-etat.fr
www.culture.gouv.fr
www.diplomatie.gouv.fr
www.elysee.fr
www.eu.int
www.g-8.de
www.insee.fr
www.nato.int
www.premier-ministre.gouv.fr
www.outre-mer.gouv.fr
www.senat.fr
www.un.org
www.wto.org

04

a snapshot of major French-speaking economies

By doing business in French, you could have access to a market of another 300 million French speakers.

Here are fact files for some of the important French-speaking economies in Europe (Belgium, Luxembourg and Switzerland) as well as for Canada.

Summary fact files for other French-speaking countries in Africa, the Americas and Australasia are available in the Reference zone.

A snapshot of Belgium

Official name	Kingdom of Belgium
	Royaume de Belgique
Borders	France, Germany, Luxembourg, Netherlands, North Sea
Capital	Brussels
Population	10.5 million
Official languages	French, Dutch, German
Currency	Euro
Time zone	GMT +1
International phone code	+32
Domain extension	.be
Main business centres	Antwerp, Brugge, Brussels, Charleroi, Gent, Liège
Top companies (2005)	Agfa-Gevaert, Almanij, Banque Nationale Belgique, Colruyt, Dexia Group, Delhaize Group, Groupe Bruxelles Lambert, Interbrew, Solvay Group, UCB

Location

Belgium is located between France (to the west), the Netherlands (to the north-east), Germany (to the east) and Luxembourg in the south-east. It has a coastline on the North Sea.

Its capital is Brussels, also known as *Bruxelles* by the French-speaking population.

Geography

Belgium is one of the smallest countries in Europe, with an area of about 30,000 km², stretching from just under 300 km from east to west to just over 200 km from north to south. It has a coastline of only 60 km along the North Sea and its main rivers are the Meuse and the Schelde. Its landscape is flat on the coast and then rises to rolling hills and the Ardennes range inland. It has a temperate climate.

Population

Its population of just over 10 million includes about 1 million nationals of other countries. Brussels has a population of nearly 1 million and Antwerp, its second city, has nearly half a million. Gent, Charleroi and Liège each have a population of around 200,000.

Language

There are three main language communities in Belgium and each represents one of the official languages. Dutch (in the north) and French (in the south) are split roughly 60:40, with a small German-speaking community of about 70,000 in the south-east of the country. English is widely spoken in Brussels.

Religion

The majority of Belgians are Roman Catholic (75 per cent) with the next most important religions being Protestantism and Islam. Some of the population declare themselves as atheist.

National identity

The Belgian national anthem is the *Brabançonne* and its motto is *L'Union fait la force* (*Eendracht maakt macht* in Dutch), which means 'Strength lies in unity'.

History

Nearly 2,000 years ago, the area of Europe that now houses Belgium was taken over by Julius Caesar and was named Gallia Belgica, after the Belgae Celtic peoples that lived there at the time.

This was the beginning of a turbulent history for the region, under the rule of many different kingdoms. With the weakening of control from Rome, power transferred to the Franks under Clovis who adopted Christianity. Belgium later fell under one of the next most important rulers in Europe, Charlemagne, who ran an empire that stretched across most of Western Europe. On his death, Belgium became divided between different kingdoms and soon Flanders started to emerge and Gent, Bruges and Ypes were fortified. In 977, the Duke of Lorraine founded Brussels. In the fourteenth century trade flourished, making the Flemish cities wealthy and powerful for a time. However, this did not last long and Belgium soon fell back under French control. Prosperity returned under the Burgundian period with Philip the Good, until the battle between Protestantism and Catholicism erupted, brought on by the rule in 1555 of King Philip of Spain. The southern part of Belgium became known as the Spanish Netherlands, with its capital in Brussels.

The country became the Austrian Netherlands in 1713, under the Utrecht Treaty. A brief period of independence occurred in 1790, until it fell back under Austrian control. It became French again following the French Revolution in 1794 and Napoleon developed industry in the region. Following his defeat in 1815, the region changed hands once again when it was claimed by the Netherlands.

A revolution took place in 1830 and Belgium became independent. On 21 July 1831 Leopold became king and this is now a National Day. During the reigns of Leopold I and Leopold II there was significant growth in the country until the two world wars. Following this period, Baudoin became King until Albert II began his reign in 1993.

Structure

Belgium is a federal parliamentary democracy under a constitutional monarch led by the Prime Minister. There are three levels of government at federal, regional and linguistic community. It has three administrative regions: Flanders, Wallonia and Brussels. There are ten provinces and almost 600 local authorities.

Economy

Manufacturing is still an important industry in the north of Belgium, along with the international banking and finance sector, which is mainly based in Brussels. Services account for nearly 75 per cent of economic activity and industry accounts for just under 25 per cent. The rest of the economy is dedicated to agriculture. The main industries are engineering and metal products, processed food and beverages, chemicals and petroleum as well as car assembly. Belgium benefits greatly from its central geographic position in Western Europe and an excellent transport network.

Belgium is a large importer as it has few natural resources itself and is a large exporter of manufactured goods. About three-quarters of its trade is within the European Union.

Belgium formed the Benelux Union with the Netherlands and Luxembourg, and then went on to be a founding member of the precursor to the European Union in 1957. The euro became the official currency of Belgium in January 2002. It is now home to the European Union and NATO, as well as the WTO (World Trade Organisation), the OECD (Organisation for Economic Co-operation and Development) and the regional headquarters of many multinational companies. It has very much become the 'capital' of Europe.

Infrastructure

Antwerp is one of Belgium's (and the world's) busiest ports, although there are other large ports in Bruges, Gent, Hasselt, Liège, Ostende and Zeebrugge. There is an international airport in Brussels.

Brussels is well connected to the European rail network and is one of the main destinations of both the pan-European Eurostar operating between London, Brussels and Paris and the Thalys running from Amsterdam to Paris. It is very well positioned in Europe and is often seen as the 'centre' of Western Europe.

More information

www.belgium.be
www.monarchie.be
www.visitbelgium.be

A snapshot of Luxembourg

Official name	Granch Duchy of Luxembourg
	Grand-Duché de Luxembourg
Borders	Belgium, France, Germany
Capital	Luxembourg City
	Luxembourg-Ville
Population	467,000
Official languages	French, German, Luxembourgish
Currency	Euro
Time zone	GMT +1
International phone code	+352
Domain extension	.lu
Main business centres	Luxembourg City, Differdange, Dudelange, Esch-sur-Alzette
Top companies	Arcelor-Mittal, Clearstream, RTL, SES Astra

Location

Luxembourg is a small landlocked country, bordered by Belgium to the north, France to the west and Germany to the east. Its capital is Luxembourg-Ville.

Geography

Luxembourg is the sixth smallest country in the world, with a surface area of about 2,500 km². At its widest point, it is just over 80 km from north to south and a little more than 50 km from east to west. It has no coast and has a temperate climate.

It is divided into two main geographic areas: to the north are the Ardennes mountains and to the south are rolling hills and farmland. Two key areas are the Moselle Valley in the east, famous for its wine, and the iron ore basin to the south-west. The four biggest rivers are the Moselle, the Sûre, the Our and the Alzette.

Population

The Grand Duchy has a population of just over 450,000, with nearly 40 per cent being part of an international community resident in Luxembourg. As such, the country prides itself on being a microcosm of Europe. The capital has a population of about 90,000, while Luxembourg's other cities are much smaller, such as Esch-sur-Alzette with a population of 28,000 and Differdange with a population of 20,000.

Language

There are three languages spoken in Luxembourg: Luxembourgish (*Lëtzebuergesch*) which became an official language in 1994, and French and German which are both officially used as administrative languages. Luxembourg is proud of its tradition of trilingualism, and on top of this English and other languages are also taught widely in schools. English is widely spoken in the capital.

Religion

Over 85 per cent of the population is Catholic and other important religions in Luxembourg include Protestantism, Islam and Orthodox Judaism.

National identity

The Luxembourg motto is in Luxembourgish and is *Mir wëlle bleiwe wat mir sin* ('We wish to remain what we are'). The national anthem is *Ons Heemecht* or *Notre Patrie* ('Our Homeland').

History

The origins of Luxembourg date back to 963, when Siegfried, an Ardennes Count, built a castle on a rock on the site of what is today Luxembourg. Over the years, this castle developed into the fortified city of Luxembourg and provided much interest from a military point of view due to its strategic position. It became known as Gibraltar of the North.

In 1354, the Count of Luxembourg became the Duke of Luxembourg and the country took on its status of a Duchy. Because of its location, it managed to resist many invasions but nonetheless the leadership of the country changed many times.

In 1443 it became part of the Netherlands and was then drawn into struggles with both the Austrian and French empires.

In 1815, the Grand Duchy of Luxembourg was created and independence and prosperity followed. However, there was soon more conflict and it was not until the Treaty of London, in 1867, that Luxembourg finally regained its independence. At this point it was declared a neutral state and began to dismantle its fortifications, and in 1890 the first Duke from the House of Nassau took to the throne.

Despite its neutrality, Luxembourg was occupied during both world wars. In 1948, it renounced its neutral status and instead joined a number of economic, political and military organizations in Europe.

It has had close economic co-operation with Belgium since 1921 and created Benelux with Belgium and the Netherlands in 1947, giving strong financial and trade links between these three countries. This proved to be the first step towards the modern-day European Union.

Structure

Luxembourg is a constitutional monarchy. The head of state is the Grand Duke and the latest monarch is SAR le Grand-Duc Henri who took over the hereditary position in 2000, being next in line for the throne in the House of Nassau. Executive power lies with the Grand Duke and a cabinet of 12 ministers, while legislative power sits with a parliament called the Chamber of Deputies.

There are three districts, 12 cantons and 116 communes. The three districts are Luxembourg, Diekirch and Grevenmacher. Of the 12 communes with city status, those with a population over 10,000 are Differdange, Dudelange, Esch-sur-Alzette and Luxembourg. Most of the other communes are small towns.

Economy

The citizens of Luxembourg have one of the highest per capita incomes of any country in the world. This economic development began in about 1850, with the discovery of iron ore and its exploitation attracted much immigration at the time and resulted in economic prosperity. The country still has a strong steel and iron sector, but it has started to decline since the mid-1970s. Luxembourg is now taking two routes – both industrial diversification (into chemicals, rubber, plastics and electrical equipment) and a move into services (which now accounts for over 80 per cent of economic activity). Hydroelectricity and satellite technology are two specialist sectors.

Luxembourg is now best known as a banking centre, where it has over 200 banks from over 25 countries around the world, encouraged by the secrecy code in the banking sector. It is seen as a tax haven and houses about 14,000 holding companies. It is one of the leading financial centres in the world and home to the Central Bank of Luxembourg. There is a strong insurance and telecommunications sector, and traditional agriculture and viticulture are also important. Tourism is a key sector too.

Luxembourg has built its modern reputation on being at the centre of European development. In 1945, it was a founding member of the United Nations and in 1948 a founding member of NATO. In 1952, Luxembourg became the headquarters of the first European Community, the European Coal and Steel Community, superseded in 1957 by the European Community. Luxembourg continues to house many of the institutions of today's European Union, including the European Court of Justice, the European Investment Bank, the European Court of Auditors, the Secretariat of the European Parliament and other services of the European Commission. Because of this, a European quarter has developed and Luxembourg is said to be the crossroads of Europe. Luxembourg has the euro as its currency.

About 25 per cent of Luxembourg's exports are steel, mostly produced by one company, Arcelor-Mittal. This global company remains the largest private employer in Luxembourg and the largest steel company in the world. Other exports include rubber products and chemicals. Its main trading partners are its immediate European neighbours, along with the UK, Italy and Spain. Since it is a small state, it is highly dependent on imports, mostly from Belgium and Germany, but also from France and increasingly from China. These imports include food and consumer goods.

Infrastructure

There is an international airport in Luxembourg, which is home to the national airline, Luxair. It is at the centre of the European rail network and the TGV Est European high-speed train from Paris opened in June 2007. As it is landlocked there are no ports, but the Moselle acts as a canal waterway.

More information

www.gouvernement.lu
www.luxembourg.co.uk
www.ont.lu
www.statec.lu
www.visitluxembourg.com

A snapshot of Switzerland

Official name	Swiss Confederation *Confoederatio Helvetica* *Confédération suisse*
Borders	France, Germany, Italy, Austria, Liechtenstein
Capital	Berne
Population	7.5 million
Official languages	French, German, Italian
Currency	Swiss franc
Time zone	GMT +1
International phone code	+41
Domain extension	.ch
Main business centres	Basel, Berne, Geneva, Lausanne, Zurich
Top companies	Adecco, Credit Suisse, Holcim, Nestlé, Novartis, Roche, Swisscom, Swiss Re, UBS, Zürich Financial Services

Location

The Swiss Confederation, also known as Switzerland or *La Suisse,* has borders with five countries: France in the west, Germany in the north, Austria and the Principality of Liechtenstein in the east and Italy in the south. Its capital since 1848 has been Berne (also spelt *Bern*), with Zurich, its biggest city, being the financial and commercial centre.

Geography

Switzerland has an area of about 40,000 km², which is about 220 km from north to south and about 350 km from east to west.

Switzerland has many mountains and lakes. The Jura mountains are to the west of the country and the Alps are to the south. Although the Matterhorn is the most famous peak in Switzerland, the Dufourspitze is the highest at just over 4,600 m. There are 140 glaciers in total, with the largest being Aletsch at 24 km long.

Many famous rivers such as the Rhine and the Rhône flow through Switzerland and into its lakes; Lake Geneva (*Lac Léman*), Lake Constance, Lake Neuchâtel, Lake Maggiore, Lake Lucerne and Lake Zurich. There are nearly 1,500 lakes in Switzerland.

Because of the diverse geography, the climate varies enormously from Arctic to Mediterranean.

Population

Switzerland has a population of nearly 7.5 million. The major cities are Zurich (with a population of 335,000), Geneva (175,000), Basel (170,000), Berne (125,000), Lausanne (128,000) and Lucerne (57,000). Cantons vary greatly in size – the canton of Zurich has over 1 million inhabitants, while others have as few as 15,000. Over 20 per cent of the population of the Swiss Confederation are nationals from other countries.

Language

There are three official languages in Switzerland: French, German, Italian and another national language, Romansh. German is most widely spoken language, with over 60 per cent of the population being only German speaking and mainly living in the north and the east. French is predominately spoken by about 20 per cent of the population to the west of Switzerland, towards the border with France. There are three cantons that are bilingual German and French. Italian is spoken in two cantons towards the southern border with Italy by about 8 per cent of the total population. Romansh or *Rumantsch* is spoken by only about 1 per cent of the population in one canton where people tend to be trilingual (also speaking German and Italian). A further 8 per cent of the population speak other languages and English is widely spoken in the cities in Switzerland.

Religion

The main religions in Switzerland are Catholicism and Protestantism, which are subscribed to by nearly 80 per cent of the population and are quite evenly split between the two. Just under 10 per cent of the population have no religion or other religions.

National identity

The motto is *Un pour tous, tous pour un* ('One for all, all for one') and the national anthem is *Contique Suisse*.

History

In 58 BC, Julius Caesar stopped the Helvetians from leaving for France by creating Helvetia. The first real foundations of current day Switzerland appeared in 1291, when three cantons around Lake Lucerne joined force. By 1513, 13 cantons had joined, forming the Old Confederation. There were many battles with neighbouring countries and also within Switzerland itself until the confederation was invaded by Napoleon and the French in 1798, ending the Old Confederation.

Full independence came in 1815, but was followed by a civil war between Catholics and Protestants in 1845. The power battles mainly concerned controlling the important communication routes across the Alps which had been in existence since prehistoric times. During this time more cantons became affiliated with the confederation.

In 1848, in a pioneering move, Switzerland became a democratic federal state. Many years of peace followed and have greatly influenced the country's heritage and culture.

Structure

Switzerland is the smallest federal state in the world, comprising 20 full cantons and six half cantons, with a central federal government which power shares between the four leading political parties. There is a Federal Council and two houses in Parliament, the National Council and the Council of States. Each canton has its own constitution, government, parliament, courts and laws, in harmony with those of the Confederation, and the state has control of issues such as foreign policy.

Switzerland is a neutral state and has been since its independence in 1815. Switzerland often acts as a mediator in world conflicts and spearheads many humanitarian efforts.

Economy

The Swiss economy has a highly-qualified labour force working in hi-tech and research industries including microtechnology, biotechnology and pharmaceuticals. It is internationally renowned for its precision engineering, as well as its global banking and insurance centre, based mainly in Zurich and Geneva. Tourism is an important sector with over 100 million visitors to the whole of the Alpine region each year.

Most people working in Switzerland are employed by small and medium-sized companies, and the country has one of the highest standards of living in the world. About 20 per cent of the workforce are foreign guest workers and the country is heavily dependent upon them.

Although the Swiss franc is the national currency, most Swiss companies will do business in euros, especially since most of their trade is with EU countries. Switzerland is not part of the European Union or the European Economic Area (EEA), but has been a member of the European Free Trade Association (EFTA) since 1959. There is much co-operation within Europe and many agreements signed between the EU and Switzerland.

Its main exports are chemicals and electronics, with just under 10 per cent of the total being watches. The main export markets are Germany, USA, France, Italy and the UK. Likewise the main imports are electronics and chemicals, which are then processed in Switzerland. The main import partners are Germany, Italy, France, Netherlands and Austria.

Infrastructure

There are a number of international airports in Switzerland, including Zurich, Geneva, and Basel-Mulhouse (operated by the French, German and Swiss). There is a sophisticated rail service operated mainly by the SBB (Swiss Federal Railways) and the Swiss government is actively encouraging train travel and investing heavily in that area. There are no ports as Switzerland is landlocked.

There are some breathtaking train journeys in Switzerland. One is the Glacier-Express from St Moritz to Zermatt across nearly

300 bridges and through nearly 100 tunnels. Others include the William Tell Express, the Bernina, the Palm and the Golden Pass Express.

Very important for the country are the Alpine passes. The first tunnel, the *Urnerloch* was built in the early 1700s and was 64 metres long and in the early 1900s the Gotthard railway tunnel was constructed which is 15 km long. The first road tunnel was the Great St Bernard, linking Switzerland and Italy. A new network of rail tunnels is planned, and the longest will be 57 km long.

More information

www.myswitzerland.com
www.swissworld.org

A snapshot of Canada

Official name	Canada
Borders	Arctic Ocean, Atlantic Ocean, Pacific Ocean, USA
Capital	Ottawa
Population	33 million
Official languages	English, French
Currency	Canadian dollar (CAD)
Time zone	Six time zones (GMT-3$\frac{1}{2}$–GMT-8)
International phone code	+1
Domain extension	.ca
Main business centres	Calgary, Edmonton, Montréal, Québec City, Toronto, Vancouver
Top companies	Bank of Montréal, Bank of Nova Scotia, BCE, Canadian Imperial Bank, EnCana, Manulife Financial, Power Corp of Canada, Royal Bank of Canada, Sun Life Financial, Thomson Corp

Location

Canada occupies most of the northern part of North America, and has borders with the USA to the south and with the US state of Alaska to the north-west. The Atlantic Ocean lies to the east and the Pacific Ocean to the west and with the Arctic Ocean to the north.

Canada's capital is Ottawa, which is only the fourth biggest city in the country.

Geography

Canada is the world's second-largest country in total area, after Russia, and the fourth largest in land area, after China, Russia and the United States. It is about 4,600 km from north to south and about 5,000 km from west to east. Its border with the USA is nearly 9,000 km, including the border with Alaska.

It is very mountainous, particularly to the west, with the famous Canadian Rockies, and Apalachian mountain range in the east. The highest peak, at nearly 6,000 metres, is Mount Logan in the Yukon.

The Great Lakes of Lake Ontario, Lake Huron and Lake Superior lie on Canada's southern border with the USA, as does Niagara Falls. There are other large lakes such as Lake Winnipeg, Great Slave Lake and Great Bear Lake. Canada's main rivers are the St Lawrence and MacKenzie and it has nearly 250,000 km of coastline.

Population

Canada has one of the lowest population densities in the world with 33 million inhabitants. About three-quarters of the population live within 160 kilometres of the US border and in the urban areas concentrated around the cities of Québec, Montréal, Ottowa in the east and Vancouver in the west, in what is called the Golden Horseshoe. The largest city is Toronto with a population of over 4.5 million, followed by Montréal (over 3 million), Vancouver (nearly 2 million), Ottawa (over 1 million), Calgary (nearly 1 million) and Québec City has just over half a million inhabitants.

Language

Canada has been a bilingual country since 1969 with the passing of the official Languages Act. There are two main language communities, with English being spoken as a first language by about 60 per cent of the population and French by about 25 per cent of the population. However, many other languages are spoken in Canada, including German (9.3 per cent), Italian (4.3 per cent) and Chinese (3.7 per cent). Interestingly, 40 per cent of the population identify themselves as Canadian.

French is important in everyday life and in business in the French-speaking areas of Québec province, where it is spoken by about 98 per cent of the population, especially in the two main cities of Montréal and Québec City. In Ontario province, there are French language rights in the legal and educational systems, whole communities are French and French is spoken instead of, or alongside, English. In Ottowa, 75 per cent of people speak English, 25 per cent speak French, and a small proportion of the population speak some German.

Religion

There is no official religion in Canada, although the last census showed that about 70 per cent of the population stated that they were either Catholic or Protestant. In some areas of the country, up to 15 per cent say that they are not religious. Many other religions are represented in Canada, including Judaism, Islam, Buddhism as well as Native American beliefs.

National identity

Its national anthem is 'O Canada' and the royal anthem is 'God save the Queen'. Its motto is *D'un océan à l'autre – A Mari Usque Ad Mare*, which means 'From sea to sea'.

History

Before 1500, Canada was inhabited by aboriginal peoples, called First Nation, and Inuit peoples. Viking invasions occurred around 1000 AD.

European explorers arrived as early as 1497 and in 1534 Jacques Cartier claimed the Gulf of St Lawrence for France. In 1583, Newfoundland became England's first colony. Both nations set up companies to exploit trade in the region: France's

New France in 1627 and Britain's Hudson Bay Company in 1670. Both now had substantial empires in North America.

Between 1756 and 1763, there was a seven-year war during which the British gained control of Québec and Montréal, finishing with the implementation of the Treaty of Paris where Britain took control of many French colonies. Further wars broke out in the early 1800s due to rebellion from the population as well as the war between the USA and Britain between 1812 and 1814.

In 1840, the Act of Union united parts of Canada to create the Province of Canada, bringing English and French-speaking communities together. The next major development towards today's Canada came in 1867 when the British North American Act created a confederation, which it named the Dominion of Canada. The final province, Newfoundland, joined in 1949.

A number of notable events took place in the intervening years, namely the Gold Rush in the Yukon in 1898, the Great Depression in 1929 and in 1967 a visit from President de Gaulle of France who famously declared *Vive le Québec libre*. From 1960 onwards there was a rise in pressure for an independent Québec. This was taken to referendum during the 1980s and 1990s when it was rejected, albeit by narrow majorities of just 1 per cent at times. Since 2006, there are moves by the government to make Québec an autonomous 'nation' within a federal Canada.

Canada has gradually gained full independence from the UK, a process which was completed in 1982, yet it remains a member of the Commonwealth.

Structure

Canada is a constitutional monarchy with Elizabeth II, Queen of Canada, as head of state. It has a federal system of parliamentary government and the Parliament consists of the Senate and the House of Commons, presided over by the Prime Minister. The legal system is based on English common law, except in Québec, where a civil law system based on French law prevails.

Canada has ten provinces – Alberta, British Columbia, Manitoba, New Brunswick, Newfoundland and Labrador, Nova Scotia, Ontario, Prince Edward Island, Québec and Saskatchewan. It also has three territories – Northwest Territories, Nunavut and Yukon Territory.

Economy

Canada is one of the world's wealthiest nations. This is mainly due to strong mining, manufacturing and service sectors. The Canadian economy is dominated by the service industries of banking, finance and insurance, which employs about three-quarters of all Canadians. Canada is one of the world's most important suppliers of agricultural products, as well as many other natural resources such as gold, nickel, aluminum and lead.

Canada is highly dependent on international trade, especially trade with the United States which accounts for about 80 per cent of its exports, mainly of machinery, equipment, automotive and other industrial goods. Its other key trading partners are Japan, the European Union, the United Kingdom and, more so, China and Mexico. Major imports come from the USA, China, Mexico, Japan and the UK. In 1989, Canada signed the Canada–US Free Trade Agreement (FTA) and in 1994, the North American Free Trade Agreement (NAFTA) (which includes Mexico). Canada has so far avoided economic recession and has maintained the best overall economic performance in the G8.

Infrastructure

There is an extensive road and rail network, which is concentrated towards the US border and in the south-east of Canada. There are some stunning rail journeys, including the Coast to Coast (Vancouver to Halifax), as well as the Rocky Mountaineer and the Polar Bear Express.

Canada's busiest ports are Vancouver, Montréal and Halifax. Canada has 30 international airports, the five busiest being Toronto, Vancouver, Montréal, Calgary and Edmonton.

More information

www.canada.gc.ca
www.canada.com
www.chamber.ca
www.statcan.ca

zone

business culture

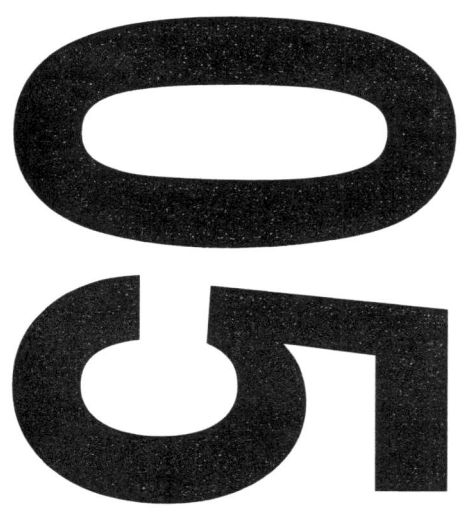

05

become a global business

You need to have a global mindset and build a global business to be successful in business overseas, irrespective of which country you are working in. Although this takes investment, the cost of losing business – or not even knowing that opportunities exist in the first place – is even greater.

Business is global

The globalization of business is well accepted and economies around the world benefit from trade between nations. Some countries could perhaps not even survive without it. Many businesses import and export and have customers across the globe. More and more companies are setting up alliances and partnerships beyond their national boundaries and more than ever, individuals are mobile in seeking out opportunities for work.

Sometimes you don't have to travel that far to see different cultures working together in different languages. In our multicultural cities, it could be that you meet, serve, work and socialize with people from many different cultures in your daily professional and social lives. London has people speaking more than 300 different languages and people from about 90 different communities working in the capital. Nearly every nation, culture and religion is represented. The same pattern can be found in the cities of New York and Toronto, as well as the European capitals of Luxembourg and Brussels.

French business is global

Business is global and this is particularly true of the French business world. France has a long history of being a trading nation through its colonies and it continues to trade across the globe with the territories of the DOM-TOMs, with francophone Africa, and nearer to home, with its neighbours in the European Union. In fact France's exports equal over 25 per cent of its GDP, and so do its imports. Furthermore, many of France's large companies are the most multinational in the world and some have over 60 per cent of their employees based outside of France. Within France, Paris is a very multicultural city with over 20 per cent of the residents in the capital having been born in other countries.

Language and cultural barriers

Surveys of UK businesses which export have shown that nearly half hit language or cultural barriers and one in five companies has stated that it has lost business as a result of meeting barriers. The actual figure may be even higher than that, as very often companies do not know why they lose business overseas or are not aware of the opportunities that they are missing due to a lack of language and cultural skills. On a national level, it can actually hamper economic growth if companies are not competitive internationally as they lose out on the potential to export to new markets.

A survey by the British Chambers of Commerce has shown that a lack of preparation, lack of knowledge and most importantly lack of confidence can lead to poor communication and leads on to a loss of business. You can come across major problems when growing your business globally in many areas. The main reasons for losing business overseas include:

- sales enquiries from phone, fax and email are not picked up or not followed up
- problems with answering phones and switchboards to non-English speakers
- delays in responding to customers and potential customers due to lack of language skills
- negotiating contracts and agreements in other languages
- problems with agents and distributors
- errors in translation and interpreting
- being unable to make good contacts at exhibitions and trade fairs
- preparing technical literature
- misunderstandings over technical details.

A lack of confidence (12 per cent) and a lack of cultural affinity (12 per cent) were two key reasons exporting companies stated for losing business. Differences in business culture can make doing business in other countries stressful. The main cultural barriers are found in the following situations:

- business etiquette
- business management style
- meetings
- social behaviour
- negotiating
- nationalism
- honesty and truth.

Advantages of language and cultural skills

However, there is a positive side to this story and the London Business Survey by CBI London highlights for the first time that foreign language skills are a key factor in business success – with 94 per cent of employers believing that these skills are important for the London economy. The British Chambers of Commerce survey went on to show that companies export more if they have language and cultural skills.

Harnessing language and cultural skills not only allows organizations and individuals to overcome barriers at work, but can even allow them to move the management of their businesses to another level by achieving a competitive advantage. Communication is key in building relationships and as such language and culture should be at the heart of any international strategy. Furthermore, you can even come to incorporate some of these ideas into your everyday management techniques and get a competitive advantage in the market.

Get a global mindset

The best thing to do is to become multicultural so you can work successfully in many cultures, French speaking or otherwise. So here is the first step on that journey.

If you have a desire to grow your business globally or if you are already implementing an international strategy, then you must declare openly that you and your business are now global. You will then think in a different way and plan things differently.

You can become aware of where differences exist and how they may impact on the business world. These differences manifest themselves as different preferences, expectations, ways of communicating, ways of negotiating, ways of running meetings, ways of shaping deals, ways of providing customer service and ways of adapting a product or service. Differences may occur in the following areas:

- asking questions
- business dress code
- criticism
- decision making
- delivery dates
- eye contact
- gift giving
- greeting colleagues
- international trade
- interruptions in meetings

- level of detail needed
- marketing
- negotiations
- overlap of business and social life
- paying invoices
- punctuality
- risk taking
- signing contracts
- terms of trade
- verbal agreements
- women in the workplace
- working hours
- work–life balance

Get a global mindset – top ten tips

Clearly there is more to getting a global mindset than working through a ten-point plan, but even just reading this page will change how you communicate with business people from other cultures and languages forever:

1 Be aware of how you react and behave, what you expect and prefer.

2 Be aware of how others may react and behave, what they may expect and prefer.

3 Be open to people of different cultures and speaking different languages.

4 Observe carefully and take your cue from your customers and colleagues.

5 Question yourself as to why things are happening in a certain way.

6 Ask your customers or colleagues about the business process in their culture – and share with them how it happens in your culture.

7 Continually research the culture of a country, be hungry for knowledge, almost to the point of obsession.

8 Spend as much time with people of that culture or in that country.

9 If you're getting out of your depth, ask for professional help.

10 Count to ten and use the time to think.

By taking this ten-point plan on board, you will learn not to jump to conclusions nor get into negative vicious circles when something doesn't quite happen as you expect.

Build a global business

Once you've prepared yourself, why not prepare your business to appeal to those in the French-speaking world?

These are some of the areas of your business that you will have to think about adapting:

- accounts department
- after-sales support
- annual report
- brochures
- business cards
- business dinners
- conferences
- customer service
- delivery
- emails
- exhibitions
- instructions
- invoices
- leaflets
- market research
- meetings
- packaging
- pricing
- proposals
- purchase orders
- reception
- sales presentations
- seminars
- social events
- switchboard
- telephone calls
- website

Build a global business – top ten tips

Again, there is much more to building a global business than a ten-point plan, but this will give you a starting point:

1 Make your English 'global English', so that it is clear and understandable by people speaking English as a second or third language.

2 Put together an international communications strategy, not only to overcome language and cultural barriers, but also to harness the power of using languages and culture to your competitive advantage.

3 Undertake a language audit to find out which language and cultural skills are available to you already and how many people speak French.

4 Create a French website to establish your presence in the French market, boost your search engine traffic and promote your business in France.

5 Tailor your marketing materials to your markets in France and other French-speaking economies, including a French business card.

6 Encourage your teams to start learning French – or to pick it back up – so they can help you to build relationships with your French-speaking customers or partners.

7 Give your team cultural training on French-speaking markets so they are confident to work with French-speaking customers or partners.

8 Begin to include recruiting people with French language skills in addition to the required technical skills for the job in hand.

9 Engage the services of a translator or interpreter to assist in sales, marketing or customer service activities if required and consider them as an extension of your team.

10 Research your market and the way of doing business in that market.

It could be that you didn't even realize that you'd lost a contract because of cultural differences, or that you'd not been asked to propose for a project, or that an agent just didn't get back to you. It could be a useful exercise to go back over your list of international leads for the last three years and, with the fresh pair of eyes that you now have, ask whether some of these business opportunities passed you by because things didn't quite turn out as you expected, because people didn't behave quite as you thought they should have or because you thought they wanted something different to what it turned out they actually wanted. And perhaps, with hindsight, you may see that you hit a language or cultural barrier and that you could have put your message across in a different way.

Being global is a different state of mind. But once you get there it is amazingly helpful and will give you an inner confidence to really make the most of your time doing international business. It will hopefully bring you many more fruitful business relationships and financially rewarding business deals.

More information

British Chambers of Commerce language survey (2004)
www.chamberonline.co.uk

CBI Survey
www.rln-london.com/pdf/pressrelease_cbilondonsurvey.pdf

CILT language skills capacity audits (2002–3)
www.cilt.org.uk

Hagen (2005), Language and culture in British business, CILT
www.cilt.org.uk

Languages at Work survey
www.languageadvantage.com

Metra Martech study (1999)
www.metra-martech.com

Talking World Class – the impact of language skills on the UK
economy Talking World Class – the impact of language skills
on the London economy
www.cilt.org.uk

UK Trade & Investment
www.uktradeinvest.gov.uk

06
getting academic

There is a whole academic discipline that explains the reasons for the similarities and differences between cultures.

More similar than different

There are bookshelves full of books and websites full of pages telling you how different it is to do business in other countries. They talk about the language and cultural barriers: what you should do, what you shouldn't do; what you should say, what you shouldn't say; about what can go wrong, how it is so hard. It is easier to dwell on what is different or 'wrong' rather than what is similar and 'right' about a situation. And let's not deny that it won't be the same as popping into your local office.

So are there other ways of looking at things? Is there a way of looking at it that gets you into a 'can do' frame of mind? Is there a way for you to engage positively and feel relaxed doing business in French-speaking countries?

Genetically speaking, we share 100 per cent of our DNA with our French-speaking colleagues and customers. So, any differences you may find between people in your country and those you meet when working in French-speaking countries across the globe are, in the greater scheme of things, pretty marginal. So let's start from the premise that all people are fairly similar.

What is more, according to Maslow's hierarchy of needs, we all need and desire the same things in life, irrespective of which culture we come from. These can be classified into five areas:

- physiological needs: this is the basic need for oxygen, food and water
- safety needs: the need to feel and be safe away from emergency or chaos
- the need for love and belonging: this is the need to give and receive love, as well having the sense of belonging
- the need for esteem: this is the point at which achievement, status, reputation and independence become important
- the need for self-actualization: the need to be able to do what you were 'born to do' and to be able to grow, find fulfilment and experience new things.

As such, people all over the world:

- have the same basic survival needs in life
- have families who they want to care for and to whom they want to give better prospects than the previous generation
- are consumers of basic goods and services, and luxuries when they can afford to

- are workers, either because they have to or because they want to
- are trading partners, for import, export, joint ventures or taking part in a global business.

Despite their similarities, every nation, culture and people of a common religion has a tendency to behave in a certain way. Even men and women have different cultures. You even find different corporate cultures within companies. There may be more than one way to get to the same end. Let's look at the concept of 'culture' in more detail so that we can begin to understand the differences between people of different cultures.

What is culture?

There are many different ways to describe culture and one of the main reasons for this is that it is actually hard to describe something that is so intrinsic and deep-seated within us.

It is something to do with how the world is perceived, how you as an individual experience life and how life is organized. It may be a way of thinking or a way of being.

Culture can be described as:

- assumptions
- behaviours
- beliefs
- customs
- ethics
- ideas
- ideals
- identity
- morals
- norms
- perceptions
- practices
- principles
- systems
- values

Getting academic

There is a whole academic discipline about managing across cultures – or the study of intercultural management or cross-cultural awareness, as it is sometimes called. It is important as, notwithstanding what we have said about everybody being mostly similar, there are proven differences between people from different cultures.

We'll give you a whistle stop tour of the key principles behind intercultural management. As this is an academic discipline, there are a number of models including:

- layers of culture also known as 'the onion'
- Geert Hofstede's theories of intercultural management
- Fons Trompenaars' theories of intercultural management.

These models will explain why there are similarities and differences between cultures and what they are.

The onion

The potential for misinterpretation of a message in your own language with people you know well is already massive. So adding in other languages and other cultures can only complicate things further and increase the potential risk of misinterpretation.

Understanding why things are the way they are helps you to set your expectations at the right level, adapt your behaviour to the current situation and ensure that your needs and preferences are communicated in an appropriate way.

You need to really stop and think about how you interpret the expectations, the preferences and the behaviour of your clients or business partners. Their messages will only be interpreted by you once you have passed them through your filtering process. Because of this, you will be 'distorting' their expectations, preferences and behaviours based upon where you are coming from. Likewise, you need to think about how your expectations, your preferences and your behaviour in a business and social environment could be interpreted by your customers, colleagues and business partners around the world, as they 'filter' your messages.

Everyone passes messages through a filtering process, which can be neatly explained by comparing culture to an onion. You don't even realize you're doing it. By understanding and acknowledging this filtering process that has been going on subconsciously for years and bringing it into your consciousness, you can start to question your own judgements when working with your international work colleagues and partners.

This filtering process – imagine an onion as you peel it – has lots of layers which can be applied in a national, regional, local, religious, business, corporate or family setting:

- the outer layer: the 'stuff' we can easily identify as part of a particular culture such as clothes, food, housing or even language
- the middle layer: norms (what is considered right and wrong) and values (what is good or bad) are not visible but influence how people behave
- inner layer: assumptions and approaches to solving problems and dilemmas.

Fons Trompenaars, a cultural guru, explains that while it is often easy to physically 'see' and become familiar with the outer layer of culture, it is possible to learn the norms and values but it will take time and understanding to become familiar with the inner layer of assumptions and basic approaches to life.

Geert Hofstede

Geert Hofstede, who is Dutch, carried out research into the preferences of a large number of employees around the world working for the company IBM.

He has produced a mapping of 50 nationalities against a number of tools he called 'dimensions'. His dimensions provide a framework for describing where differences in culture exist and how to explain and predict behaviour so that you can become more effective in dealing with people in other countries.

The four original dimensions include: power distance, uncertainty avoidance, individualism-collectivism, masculinity-feminism and he later added a fifth dimension – long-term short-term orientation:

1 **Power distance** looks at the degree to which an employee will accept that a superior has more power than he/she does just because he/she is the boss. It is a measure of power and inequality.

2 **Uncertainty avoidance** looks at the ability of a culture to live without formal rules and to live with ambiguity. It measures how much structure a society needs.

3 **Individualism-collectivism** shows the degree of concern an employee is likely to have for himself as an individual over the group as a whole. It is a measure of how group-oriented an individual may be.

4 **Masculinity-femininity** describes whether a culture is likely to tend towards a male culture (work goals, assertiveness, male roles) or towards a more female culture (personal goals, nurturing, female roles). It is a measure of the role of males and females in society.

5 **Long-term short-term orientation** describes the view that an individual may take regarding time.

Mappings against these dimensions exist for the French-speaking nations of France, Belgium, Canada, Switzerland and West Africa and can be compared to the English-speaking nations of the UK, USA and Ireland. It can be an indicator of how 'alien' a particular culture may feel in each of the areas discussed. We will look at these results further in the French business zone.

Fons Trompenaars

Meanwhile Fons Trompenaars, along with Charles Hampden-Turner, developed a similar, but alternative model over ten years by interviewing over 15,000 managers in nearly 30 countries.

This model has seven dimensions:

1 **universalism vs. particularism** (rules or relationships)
2 **individualism vs. collectivism** (individual or group)
3 **affective vs. neutral** (emotional or non-emotional)
4 **diffuse vs. specific** (involvement or non-involvement)
5 **achievement vs. ascription** (prove ourselves to receive status or it is given to us)
6 **sequential vs. synchronic** (one at a time or several things at once)
7 **internal vs. external** (control environment or it controls us).

Trompenaars provided analysis for France, Belgium and Switzerland and for the English-speaking countries of the UK and the USA. Again, we will look at these in the French business zone.

Geert Hofstede and Fons Trompenaars carried out extensive research and created many methodologies and tools to analyse culture. This short overview provides you with just a glimpse. We hope it will get you on the road to fathoming out this massive but so important subject of managing across cultures. There is more information and a reading list in the Reference zone. It is worth your while to read more as it can help you to really get to know how to manage across cultures to your competitive advantage.

More information

Fons Trompenaars **www.7d-culture.nl**

Geert Hofstede **www.geert-hofstede.com**

Maslow hierarchy of needs **www.maslow.com**

zone

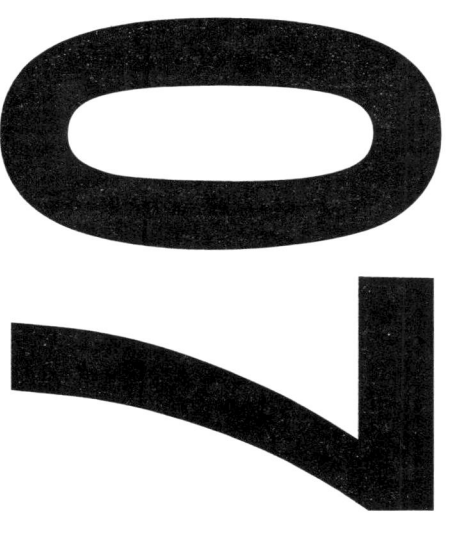

French business culture

France is said to have one of the highest cultural barriers for UK businesses.

France is said to have one of the highest language and cultural barriers for UK companies, despite it being one of the nearest export markets and French being taught widely in schools. This is partly due to the strong preference for the French to conduct business in French, but also due to the differences in business culture. Companies facing cultural barriers state that France is only second to Japan in terms of difficulty of doing business.

It is therefore important to understand the origins of some of the main characteristics of French business culture to help to shed light on why these differences exist and where these differences lie. It is about finding the essence of what the nation, its economy, its business structures and its people are about. It's about knowing the country and how it works intimately. It will allow you to understand how to be successful in French-speaking markets around the world.

What is French culture?

There is a common theme through many of the values that underpin French culture based on *la grandeur de la France*.

> '**France remains faithful to the great republican principles set out in the philosophy of the Age of Enlightenment and the 1789 Revolution. These principles are liberty, equality and fraternity for all of humanity. These ideals still inspire France's fight for a peaceful world that is fairer and more caring, attentive to people's aspirations and respectful of their cultures and their natural heritage.'**
>
> **Source: www.diplomatie.gouv.fr**

The arrival of a new President is always a great time for great speeches and we were not to be disappointed with the arrival of Sarkozy in 2007. In his inaugural speech he claimed that he would defend the independence and the identity of France.

Sarkozy talked also of the French as *un grand peuple* and of the country having *une grande histoire* with *la force de transformer le monde*. The French are very proud of being French and believe that the French have the best way of going about things and that other parts of the world can still learn from them. It is crucial to understand the origins of these claims to completely understand the French culture – and its subsequent impact on the French business culture.

Pinpointing French culture is never an easy job, mostly because it is so full of contradictions. Sarkozy spoke about some of these creative tensions in his opening speech:

> « *La France ... qui veut l'ordre mais qui veut aussi le mouvement, qui veut le progrès mais qui veut la fraternité, qui veut l'efficacité mais qui veut la justice, qui veut l'identité mais qui veut l'ouverture.* »
>
> **Source: www.sarkozy.fr**

Even though France is currently facing many social and economic issues at home and internationally, it remains true to its belief that France is one of the greatest democratic nations on earth as it sets off on its path of reform.

The president was keen to improve relationships with the USA and stated: 'I want to tell them that France will always be by their side when they need her, but that friendship is also accepting the fact that friends can think differently.'

He was also keen to form a link between Europe and Africa by building a 'Mediterranean Union' as well as playing a central role in remodelling the so far failed European Constitution, so that European integration could progress, albeit in a different direction given France's rejection of the referendum in 2005. Sarkozy is not keen to expand the European Union beyond its current 27 members and is openly opposed to Turkey becoming a member of the EU.

Sarkozy is acutely aware of the changing structure of the business world and is keen to forge links with the emerging super-economies of Brazil, Russia, China and India.

Origins of French characteristics

There are many ways of describing France and the French. We have picked out some of the key characteristics to give you some further insights French culture. Each characteristic has a different origin – it may have been influenced by events in France's history or by its geography, economics or politics. If you understand some of these tendencies, you will soon see why things are as they are today, and it will be easier to understand expectations and behaviour that stem from them.

These words are commonly used to describe different aspects of French business life and have a high impact on the French business world today. Many of the words we have come across may be impressions rather than fact and may even be opposing, which shows how complex it can be to actually define a nation and its people – and that France is a country of contradictions.

Table 5: words to describe French business culture

nationalistic, patriotic, protectionist **Impact on business:** do business the French way	There are many strong symbols of French identity, the most striking of which must be the motto *liberté, egalité, fraternité* (for all). All of this gives rise to strong patriotism and shared values within France, illustrating what the French Republic stands for and what it will defend. The French are, and always have been, very proud of being French. They continue to put the French language and the French culture at the centre of everything they do.
ethnically diverse, global outlook, influential, tolerant **Impact on business:** French business is very outward-looking and international	France has been a secular state since 1882, allowing the existence of all faiths and beliefs. The separation of the State from the Church in 1905 gave rise to the principle of *laïcité*, which includes the freedom to practise any religion within France, as well as the State having no formal ties with any particular religious group. There are three other forces at play here too. There was massive immigration to help

out with the war effort and to rebuild France in the post-war period. France's expansion into the francophone world and the French colonies has always meant that it has had a very outward-looking trade and foreign policy. Respect for human rights, respect for democratic principles, respect for law and co-operation between nations has put it at the centre of the international community.

agricultural,
family-oriented,
regional,
rural

Impact on business:
French business is still very much focused on Paris

80 per cent of France's mainland is rural and as such it has a very strong political lobby from the populations living and working in the regions. These areas often have a strong cultural identity and even a local language. France is still very much focused on family culture and has many family businesses. Many French companies are still based in and around Paris and the Île-de-France region, which also provides the largest concentration of consumers too. Other business centres are emerging such as Toulouse for aeronautical industries. The major divisions are north/south (historically Germanic vs. Mediterranean) and east/west (industrialized vs. seafaring/ agricultural).

elegant,
elitist, fashionable,
sophisticated

Impact on business:
presentation, status and connections are important in French business

There has always been a dichotomy between the France of the regions and Paris. Traditionally, Parisians were seen as the educated tier of society. With it came images of the French being intelligent and spirited with elegance and sophistication. Many key positions in the French government, business and finance sectors are held by the French aristocracy and graduates from the *Grandes Écoles*. This is one of the most important elements of integrating into the French business scene.

bureaucratic,
centralized,
hierarchical,
regulated

Impact on business:
French business can be very hierarchical and bureaucratic at times

In the early 1800s Napoleon tried to control his empire from Paris. Although there is no doubting that this was about control, more positively, it was also to encourage justice and education for all. This was summed up in this quote: 'They waver between liberalism, in the name of freedom of thought, and demanding regulation to enforce republican values' (www.diplomatie.gouv.fr). Furthermore, centralized political, administrative and education systems have greatly influenced the way that businesses are run in France, making them highly-planned with clear hierarchies and defined roles. The business environment is still relatively regulated too.

debating,
intellectual,
rational,
technocratic

Impact on business:
ideas and proposals must be presented in a very logical way

Because of the high value placed on a rigorous academic qualifications and the structure of the Grandes Écoles, technical degrees are very well regarded. With this comes the rational thinking and open debating which is part of the national culture. Philosophy is also taught throughout the French education system. Hard sales techniques are unlikely to work.

bold,
innovative,
inventive,
progressive

Impact on business:
French business can
be very innovative

France has always had the ability to sign up to a longer-term vision. This has allowed it the space to be bold and progressive and it is famous for its *grands projets* – its many groundbreaking national projects which have emerged from the country in the twentieth and twenty-first centuries, such as Concorde, the Channel Tunnel, *la Pyramide du Louvre*, the Pompidou Centre, *La Grande Arche de la Défense*, Ariane rockets and the continued development of nuclear energy. Although rigid and planned, France's industry can be extremely creative and inventive (take the aerospace industry, the fashion industry and the media sector as examples).

Business culture in other French-speaking economies

It is impossible to define a French business culture that exists across all French-speaking countries and territories of the world.

The most important concentrations of consumers are in Europe, North America and West Africa, and you will find very different business cultures in all three areas. Moreover, in large corporate or international organizations, the organizational or corporate culture often overrides the national culture. Without doubt, business cultures are converging to some extent, but whether there is an international business model taking the best of what the world has to offer, or if it is an adaptation of the Anglo-Saxon business model, only time will tell. What is certain is that strong business cultures exist in most of the French-speaking countries and what unites the French-speaking countries is *la Francophonie*.

Belgium and Luxembourg

The business culture in Belgium and Luxembourg is very similar to that of France, although there is the influence of a more direct business style of the Flemish and German populations in Belgium. Also, both Brussels and Luxembourg City are very cosmopolitan international business centres, and as such they tend to have a more open business culture and a high level of sophistication in their markets.

Switzerland

The French-speaking population will carry out business in a very similar way to that in France. Again there will be a huge influence from the direct business style of the Germanic business culture.

Canada

Canadian business culture is strongly influenced by US culture and the Anglo-Saxon way of life, albeit slightly tamed. There is a view that business in French-speaking Canada is an American business culture, but carried out in French, giving consumers access to two distinct cultures.

Africa

The pace of doing business in most parts of Africa is generally much slower. Economies and administrations are not always stable, and consumers' expectations can be different. There is a completely different way of doing business in Africa and building personal relationships forms a major part of everyday business life.

Key areas of differences in culture

The main differences between the key French-speaking countries and the UK and the USA according to the Hofstede analysis were in the areas of power distance and uncertainty avoidance:

- **Power distance** – France, Belgium and West Africa tend to have a high power distance, meaning that they are hierarchical cultures, while the English-speaking countries along with Canada and Switzerland tend to have low power distance cultures. This is likely to lead to one of the biggest differences you may notice in doing business in some of the French-speaking countries.
- **Uncertainty avoidance** – Belgium and France scored very highly on uncertainty avoidance, meaning that they tend to be very structured cultures which need rules. Switzerland and West Africa also scored highly, while Canada, the USA, the UK and Ireland had low uncertainty avoidance. Again, this is likely to be one of the big areas of difference when doing business in France.

According to the Trompenaars analysis, the main differences lie in the areas of individualism-collectivism and neutral-affective:

- **Individualism-collectivism** – the USA is very individualistic, while France was at the opposite end of the scale being very collective. Switzerland and Belgium were centred about the midpoint, along with the UK. This means that Americans doing business with the French will need to appreciate the more 'consensual' way of doing business.
- **Neutral-affective** – the UK has been shown to be very neutral and non-emotional. Belgium, France and the USA are centred around the midpoint between each extreme. This will therefore be the biggest area of difference for British people doing business in France.

More information

Fons Trompenaars: **www.7d-culture.nl**

Geert Hofstede: **www.geert-hofstede.com**

Managing Cultural Differences Lisa Hoecklin

Sarkozy speech in English: **www.ambafrance-uk.org**

Sarkozy speech in French: **www.elysee.fr,
www.diplomatie.gouv.fr,** or **www.sarkosy.fr**

08

French business language

French is still widely used as a business and intermediary language in francophone countries and will be the language of preference if there is no-one English speaking present in a meeting or a multicultural team.

Use of French in business in France

The use of French in business has real implications for overseas businesses wanting to do business in France. While some may feel able to use English in business situations in France, the best advice is plan to conduct all meetings and presentations in French. This will, of course, make your product or service more appealing to French-speaking customers. In some situations, it is actually compulsory to use French.

Here are some areas to consider:

- use of French language on the internet
- use of French language in audiovisual
- use of French in advertising
- use of French on packaging
- use of French in instruction manuals
- use of French on signs
- providing customer service.

The *Toubon* law of 4 August 1994 was introduced to protect French consumers (and superseded the *Bas-Lauriol* law), stating that French is the *langue du travail*. This law forbids the sale of 'goods and services' in France exclusively in a foreign language and insists that government communication with the French public is in French. It applies as much to advertising as it does to invoicing. In reality, you may find dual-language marketing materials, or even translated footnotes in French.

Use of French in business in Belgium

You need to take care in Belgium about making your language choice as it is still a sensitive issue. If you are not sure whether the mother tongue of your client or business partner is French or Flemish, then use English in the first instance. In Brussels, English would be acceptable as a common language for business.

Use of French in business in Luxembourg

Luxembourgish is the daily spoken language for most people in the country at all levels of society. However, it is not widely used to explain more complex or conceptual ideas, so German and French both tend to be widely used in the media and in political and religious life. However, French is the official language of the administration, jurisdiction and largely for parliament too. Public services are expected, when possible, to respond in the language in which they are addressed. Official public documents are often produced in Spanish and Portuguese too due to the high proportion of these communities in Luxembourg. Because it is such an international city, English would be acceptable for business in Luxembourg Ville.

Use of French in business in Switzerland

The Swiss tend not to speak all four languages. It is becoming more likely that they speak their mother tongue and English and only understand one of the other languages of their country. The German spoken in Switzerland is Swiss German and the French spoken is largely similar to that spoken in France.

In business, people often speak in their mother tongue, and it is assumed that they understand the language of their colleagues. The exception is Italian and Rumantsch speakers, who tend to switch to French or German. More and more, people speak English as a common language.

Most products in the stores are labelled in German, French and Italian, or at least in German and French. All official documents are issued in the mother tongues of the population. A lot of money is spent on translations in both the public and private sectors. English is becoming more and more dominant and being used more and more for advertising campaigns as it has prestige appeal, and on a practical level, can be used across Switzerland.

Use of French in business in Canada

The language issues in Canada are spearheaded by the *OQLF*. It will provide support 'so that French is the usual and normal language of work, communications, trade and businesses in the Administration and companies' and will point out where French needs to be used and how to use it correctly. Language regulations have been made law, such as in 1993, when it was modified to state that French be 'markedly predominant' on exterior business signs. The *OQLF* does have the power to fine businesses and every year receives thousands of complaints that only English has been used for instructions, business signs, websites, customer service and advertisements.

Use of English in French Business

French business language has adopted many words from global English that are in everyday use in workplaces around the world. However, the *Académie française* has an official list of the 'proper' French words that you could be using instead.

Table 6: examples of English business words in use in business French

email	*courriel*
newsletter	*lettre d'information, infolettre*
spam	*pourriel, pollupostage*
messenger	*messager, messagerie instantanée*
chatroom	*salon, forum, bavardoire*
chat	*tchatcher, dialogue en ligne, clavardage*
news	*nouvelles, infos, actualités*
home	*accueil, page d'accueil*
podcasting	*diffusion pour baladeur, baladodiffusion*
job	*travail, emploi*

There are no tremendous differences between the French business language in use in France, Belgium, Luxembourg and Switzerland.

Differences in business writing

There are a few differences in writing practices in French which include adding a space before punctuation marks (e.g. _ ?, _ !) and using <<_>> as speech marks. Data is written with commas rather than decimal places so 12,3 rather than 12.3 and for larger numbers, with spaces so 123 456 rather than 123,456. You can also set your word processing package to spell check in French and insert accents by using the Insert Symbol command in Microsoft software.

More information

www.academie-francaise.fr/dictionnaire
www.diplomatie.gouv.fr
www.legifrance.gouv.fr
www.oqlf.gouv.qc.ca/ressources/gdt.html
www.swissworld.org

09 French business environment

This section will give you the knowledge you need about the economic and business environment in France at the current time.

France has developed its economy and business structure in line with many of the Western European nations. Here are the key events:

Table 7: defining moments in the economic development of France

1795	The franc becomes the official currency of France.
1864	The right to strike is granted.
1895	The CGT union is established.
1930	The creation of *assurances sociales*.
1945	France joins the UN.
1945	The creation of social security and *comité d'enterprise*.
1948	The Treaty of Brussels creates the Western Union.
1949	France joins the North Atlantic Treaty Organization.
1950	The introduction of SMIG (*le salaire minimum interprofessionnel garanti*).
1952	The Treaty of Paris comes into force, establishing the European Coal & Steel Union.
1954	France joins the Western European Union.
1958	The Treaty of Rome is signed and France becomes a founding member of European Economic Community.
1960	The new franc is introduced.
1968	France experiences a social revolution (May).
1970	The introduction of the mimimum wage – *SMIC (le salaire minimum interprofessionnel de croissance)*.
1975	France joins the G6.
1976	The G7 is established.
1993	European Union founded after the signing of the Maastricht Treaty.
1995	Chirac accepts that France will be an integral part of NATO.
1995	France joins the WTO.
1997	The G8 comes into being.
1999	The introduction of the euro.
2000	European stock exchange Euronext starts.
2002	The euro becomes the sole currency.
2007	Euronext merges with NYSE.

Here is an overview of the key business structures that you need to help you do business successfully in France.

Chambers of Commerce

The French Chambers of Commerce and Industry (CCI) are an important part of business life in France. There are over 150 chambers representing 1,800,000 French companies. They are a great source of information, giving a good understanding on how to do business in France.

Comité d'entreprise

A *comité d'entreprise* is compulsory for companies with over 50 employees and was created in 1945. It is a communication tool between employees and management and provides a consultation role for key decisions to be made through monthly meetings, which are required by law.

Companies

There are about 2,000 national companies in France and some of the world's most successful multinationals are French. Some of its companies are world famous, such as Michelin, Christian Dior, Renault and Peugeot, while others are world leaders in their field (e.g. Saint-Gobain). The biggest company in France by revenue is Total, the oil company, and it is also one of the largest employers. Many of the state-run organizations in France are massive employers such as the civil service and *la Poste*, as are some of the global companies, such as Fedex, McDonald's, Johnson, Microsoft and Pepsi. A list of top French-speaking companies is available in the Reference zone.

However, a large part of the French business community is made up of small and medium-sized enterprises (SMEs) and it is estimated that there are about 2.5 million of these companies in France, with a high proportion of these being family businesses. In fact, about 10 million people are employed by small and medium-sized companies below 250 employees and 6 million by larger companies.

Company registration

Setting up a company in France can be more expensive and more time consuming than in your country, so be sure to allow additional time for company registration. French companies in metropolitan France or in the overseas departments must be listed on the official French company register – *SIRENE* (*Système Informatique pour le Répertoire des Entreprises et de leurs Établissements*). Overseas companies that have representation or business activity in France must also be registered.

Companies can take on various legal forms including:

- *L'entreprise individuelle* – this is the equivalent of being self-employed.
- *La société en nom collectif* (*SNC*) – still technically self-employed but profits are shared between partners.
- *La société à responsabilité limitée* (*SARL*) – mostly adopted by *SMEs* and family businesses.
- *L'entreprise unipersonnelle à responsabilité limitée* (*EURL*) – for small companies as a variation of the *SARL* with just one director.
- *La société anonyme* (*SA*) – this structure is used by larger companies with at least seven shareholders and has limited liability.

Copyright

This is more commonly known as the *droit d'auteur* in France and is strictly implemented. It is defined by the *code de la propriété intellectuelle* and has been harmonized with European and international systems.

Data protection

The law of *Informatique et Libertés* of 1978 and 2004 give individuals the right of access to their personal information. This puts an obligation on companies that are processing personal information to register with *La Commission Nationale de l'Informatique et des Libertés*.

Government

The Ministers responsible for the business world in France hold posts that can change under different presidencies and governments, but which can include:

- Minister for the Economy, Finance and Industry (**www.minefi.gouv.fr**)
- Minister for Small and Medium-sized Enterprises, Trade, Small-Scale Industry and the Professions (**www.pme.gouv.fr**)
- Minister Delegate for Foreign Trade (**www.commerce-exterieur.gouv.fr**) supported by the large network of French embassies around the world.

Intellectual property

A trademark or new invention can be registered with the *Institut national de la propriété industrielle* where a certificate will be issued. Another route is *l'enveloppe Soleau* which enables you to lodge the date at which your work or invention came into being, but it does not accord you any protection for your idea. This is an area that is likely to need professional advice.

Judicial system

The French judicial system is based upon the 'guardian of individual liberty' (from article 66 of the Constitution). There is a two-tier system which distinguishes between ordinary courts, which deal with disputes between private individuals or bodies, and administrative courts which have jurisdiction in disputes between citizens and public authorities.

Within the ordinary courts there are civil courts and criminal courts. The civil courts are organized on a regional basis with a series of specialized courts for commercial, social security and industrial relations. The criminal courts operate at three levels for petty offences, substantial offences and serious offences, which are dealt with by the Assize Court. There is also a Youth Court, for both civil and criminal cases. For business affairs, the *Code du commerce* and *Code du travail* are important.

The highest judicial body is the *Cour de Cassation* which is responsible for examining rights to appeal and the *Conseil d'État* which is the supreme administrative court and court of final appeal on the legality of administrative acts. The government also consults the *Conseil d'État* on draft legislation and on draft orders as required.

Minimum wage

The minimum wage is a guaranteed monthly minimum wage and is called the *SMIC* (*salaire minimum interprofessionel de croissance*). In 2006, the hourly gross wage was €8.27 an hour.

Recruitment

Education is free in France and begins at the age of 6 in *maternelle* and ends at age 16. The French education system is highly centralized and students in a particular year in each school in France will be learning the same subject at the same time on any given day. There is a private education sector, which is dominated by Roman Catholic schools. The main qualifications from the French education system are the *baccaleuréat* at age 18 and then later at university, a *diplôme*, *licence* and *maîtrise*.

The higher education system in France is well developed with nearly 100 state universities. The most distinctive part of the higher education system are the *Grandes Écoles* which produce some of France's elite graduates in subjects such as engineering, law and finance. They tend to go on and take up positions in the administration and the top companies, operating a strong alumni network. It also has strong engineering and business schools, including the well-known INSEAD.

Social security

Most social security funds come from mandatory contributions from employers and employees. The remaining amount comes from specific taxes such as the CSG (*Contribution sociale généralisée* – a social security contribution levied on virtually all sources of income) or the CRDS (*Contribution pour le remboursement de la dette sociale* – a contribution to the repayment of the social debt). The French social security system is very generous by today's standards.

Stock exchange

The stock exchange (*la Bourse*) is based is Paris in the pan-European Euronext, which also has subsidiaries in Belgium, Netherlands, Portugal and the UK. It has now merged with the New York Stock Exchange (NYSE) and has become the first truly global stock exchange, trading for 21 hours a day, with seven exchanges, six countries and over two continents. It is estimated to be the fifth largest stock exchange in the world. There are a number of indices including the CAC40 (*Cotation Assistée en Continu*) and the SB120 (*Société des Bourses Françaises*).

Tax

There are a number of different taxes in France, the most important being:

- income tax – *Impôt sur le Revenu*
- company tax – *Impôt sur les Sociétés*
- social contributions – *CSG* and *CRDS*
- wealth tax – *Impôt de Solidarité sur la Fortune*
- inheritance tax – *Droits de Succession*
- sales tax – *TVA*.

There are also a number of local taxes including property tax (*Taxe Foncière*) and community charge (*Taxe d'Habitation*).

France has a number of tax treaties with other countries, as well as tax credits and allowances. An annual tax return (*Déclaration de revenus*) has to be submitted.

Telecoms and the internet

The *Minitel* system has been in existence since 1982 and was effectively a precursor to the internet, allowing users to look up telephone numbers and make simple reservations and payments 'on-line'. There were about 13 million terminals (2005) and 25 million users by 2000. By consequence, there was a lower internet penetration rate initially as French consumers did not see the need to move to the worldwide web from Minitel.

Now about 80 per cent of French people use computers at work and nearly 50 per cent of French households now own one. Internet usage has grown rapidly in line with global trends and nearly all businesses have a website now. High-speed internet, mobile phones and e-commerce are all very popular.

Trade unions

Under 10 per cent (2 million) of the working population in France is actually a member of a union and most of these are within the manufacturing and transport sectors. Although the impression is of a much higher percentage, usually through international media coverage of strikes in France, it is in fact the lowest percentage in the European Union. The origins of this perception could lie with the fact that an individual has the right to strike (*le droit de grève*) in France.

The main trade unions are:

- CGT (*Confédération Générale du Travail*).
- CFDT (*Confédération Française Démocratique du Travail*).
- FO (*Force Ouvrière*).
- CFTC (*Confédération Française des Travailleurs Chrétiens*).
- FSU (*Fédération Syndicale Unitaire*).

Website registration

AFNIC (*Association Française pour le Nommage Internet en Coopération*) is the registry of the database of *.fr* (France) and *.re* (Reunion Island) internet domain names. Since June 2006, all adults with a postal address in France can register a domain name. Before this, it was only professionals, associations or public bodies who were able to register.

Working hours

From 2000, the French working week was shortened to an average of 35 hours in an attempt to encourage job creation. However, it is now likely that it will be increased back up to 39 hours, with paid holiday of five weeks a year. The French place a great importance on taking a family holiday, usually in France, during August and much French business, outside the tourism industry, tends to slow down – if not shut down – during the summer. Business hours are generally from 8.30 a.m. to 6 or 7 p.m., traditionally with a longer break for lunch. Although this is changing in larger corporations, it is still prevalent in smaller and family-run companies.

More information

This is just a whistle stop tour of the key elements of the French business environment that you may need to consider when doing business in France. Take time to research areas of particular interest or importance to your business further.

www.acfci.cci.fr
www.afnic.fr
www.ccip.fr
www.cnil.fr
www.diplomatie.gouv.fr
www.douane.gouv.fr
www.entreprises.minefi.gouv.fr
www.eurofound.europa.eu
www.impots.gouv.fr
www.industrie.gouv.fr
www.inpi.fr
www.insee.fr
www.justice.gouv.fr
www.legifrance.gouv.fr
www.minitel.fr
www.pme.gouv.fr
www.pme.gouv.fr/formations
www.sirene.tm.fr

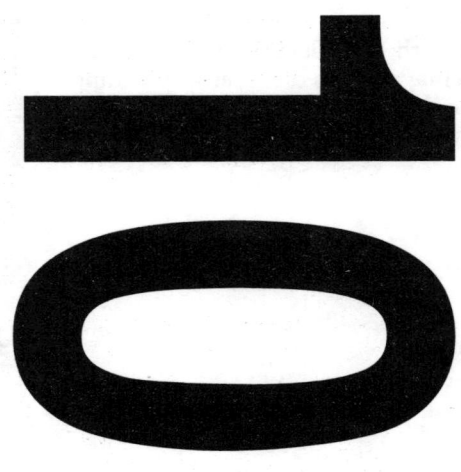

10

working in France

Essential hints and tips about
working in the French
business culture.

When you are working in France you may notice a difference between the French business culture and your own business culture. We have explored some of the reasons why this may be, and this section tells you more about how to handle these situations. If in doubt, do not be afraid to ask your business partners how things work or watch carefully for a while and take a cue from them.

Body language

Body language will be relatively similar in France, although you are likely to get less personal space than you are used to. The French are likely to stand closer, offer more physical contact and be more expressive with more shrugging, nodding and use of hands while speaking. However, in important business situations, you may find that your colleagues are very formal and 'statesman-like'.

Contracts

The French legal system relies heavily on *codes* and the most important ones for business are the *code du travail* and the *code du commerce*. There are strong labour laws, so it is prudent to take advice before entering into any contract in France.

Decision making

The French are prepared to invest time and take a longer-term view. Because of this, any decisions may take time and only come after you have been asked to supply additional information. Decisions tend to be taken by the most senior executive in the hierarchy, who may or may not be present at sales meetings and presentations. It is important therefore that your written documentation is well laid out and left with your potential customer.

Dress code

The dress code in France will be heavily dependent upon the sector in which you are working. Media, fashion and internet technology companies are more likely to be informal and 'dress down'. They may go as far as (smart) jeans and perhaps a smart jacket. If working with one of the French government departments or more traditional companies, then it would be safer to wear a dark suit. The French are known for being stylish and you should invest in a good quality designer suit. Status is still accorded based upon dress to a certain extent. Leisurewear will be more informal, but still quite smart by most standards. If you are invited to a formal event, then full eveningwear and dinner jackets should be worn.

Gift giving

You may like to give a gift to your business colleagues or partners at Christmas time, but it would not be expected each time you visit their company on formal business. However, if you are fortunate enough to be invited to dinner at home with your French business partners, then you should take a gift (but not wine as the host will provide this and not chrysanthemums as they are the flowers commonly used at funerals). If you are given a gift, it would be polite to follow-up with a thank you note. Seasonal greeting cards are sent in the New Year in France, rather than at Christmas time.

Greetings

Again this depends on the business sector in which you are working. But as a general rule, you should stick to the formal Monsieur and Madame and using *vous* until you are invited to use first names and *tu*. This is the most important area in which to follow the lead of your colleague, client or business partners. It is commonplace for there to be a handshake every time you meet someone and once people become more familiar, then there will be the kissing on the cheeks either two, three or four times, depending on where in France your clients live.

Humour

The French do enjoy some humour in certain business scenarios, but this is more likely to be once you have established a firm relationship with them. The English sarcastic sense of humour rarely translates well into other languages and cultures and this is true with French speakers too.

Management

PDGs and directors are usually strong leaders, as well as being experts in their field too, keeping abreast of technical detail and knowing plans 'inside out' in many cases. This is needed to gain the respect of the rest of the team.

Reporting lines are usually very hierarchical, with formal reporting lines running vertically. Clear responsibilities are assigned at each 'level' of the hierarchy with a 'functional' organization structure with co-ordination happening from the centre.

This type of system is heavily reliant on rules, regulations, processes and procedures, meaning it can work extremely well, but on the down side it can be slow to resolve issues as they work their way back up the line of control. In reality, employees often become creative in organizations managed in this way, working around the rules and building personal relationships within the organization to resolve issues and agree changes informally before presenting them formally.

Meetings

Meetings are likely to run quite formally with a formal agenda and serve to give information and co-ordinate resources. It is important to be well-prepared – or even over-prepared – as there is likely to be a good examination of any ideas, concepts or proposals, looking from all angles. There is unlikely to be much public disagreement in the meeting as informal discussion is likely to have been held before the meeting – or will take place afterwards. It can be useful to get to know your key clients before a meeting either remotely by email or telephone or in person and sound out your ideas.

Negotiating

Negotiations in France are more reliant on building well-presented ideas and solutions and finding a 'meeting of minds', rather than trying to 'clinch a deal'. It means that you should be more ready to use persuasion and debating skills rather than entering into hard negotiations, which can be seen as confrontational.

Networking

Many of the leaders of government, finance and business are well connected through their alumni networks from the *Grandes Écoles*. There is an elite minority who are in positions of power and influence in France, many of whom sit on each other's company boards as non-executive directors. It is this strong internal web of relationships and close working between companies that sometimes makes France a hard market to crack for overseas companies and can pose some of the largest barriers. However, if you manage either to make a contact through this network and can start to count on recommendations, or convince of the merits of your product or service, you will make good progress doing business in France.

Planning

The French business environment tends to encourage a long-term view and many *grand projets* would not have been achieved with a short-term planning horizon. Planning is usually driven by a vision of the future and plans detailing how this can be achieved are then filled in.

Sales

The French tend to take a longer-term view and will be looking to build a relationship with you. For this reason, it is important that you also take a longer-term view on how your business relationship may develop. Clearly present the rationale and benefits of your goods or services, incorporating logical arguments and setting out the return on investment. Make sure you are well prepared and have done your research. Bring back-up information as the French like to look at things from every angle and there is likely to be much discussion around any proposal you may put forward. The sales process will be serious and business-focused.

Socializing

The French are good conversationalists and love to debate topics such as world affairs, politics and more intellectual subjects such as philosophy which is an integral part of the French education system. There will be plenty of opportunity to discuss personal and family affairs, but this tends to happen further on in the relationship. A typical pattern may be to be invited for a coffee, then a lunch in a restaurant, an evening meal in a restaurant and then finally to be invited to the family home. It is far more common for wine to be served with meals at any time during the working day.

Timekeeping

It is good practice to turn up on time for a business meeting, but it would not be regarded as disrespectful to be up to 15 minutes late. Business life becomes more relaxed in the south of France – but of course we would not advise you to be late.

Trust

It is key to build up trust with your business partners or customers. This may be a slow process of building credibility while you establish your status, intelligence and expert knowledge. This process is slow as this trust has to be earnt by you by investing in the relationship.

Women

As a businesswoman, you may be treated with special respect by men in France, both in business and social situations. This is meant to be perceived as an honour, not as a means of undermining your position.

French women are now achieving higher ranks in government and commerce but still face challenges in achieving positions and levels of income that are comparable with those of men. In France, most people with significant careers in business or government are products of the exclusive *Grandes Écoles*. It is only in the past 20 years that women's enrolment in these exclusive schools has become significant.

reference zone

A: country fact files

Key facts about 20 of the largest countries in the French-speaking world, many with the fastest growing populations in the world.* These are potential French-speaking consumer markets of the future.

* Key facts about France, Belgium, Canada, Luxembourg and Switzerland are listed in the Knowledge zone.

Map 3: French-speaking Africa

Benin at a glance

Official name	The Republic of Benin *La République du Bénin*
Borders	Burkina Faso, Nigeria, Niger, Togo
Capital	Porto-Novo
Population	9 million
Official languages	French (official), Fon, Yoruba and other local languages
Currency	Franc CFA
Time zone	GMT +1
International phone code	+229
Domain extension	.bj
Main business sectors	cotton, palm oil
Main cities	Abomey, Cotonou, Parakou
National website	www.benintourisme.com

Burkina Faso at a glance

Official name	Burkina Faso
Borders	Benin, Côte d'Ivoire, Ghana, Mali, Niger, Togo
Capital	Ouagadougou
Population	14.7 million
Official languages	French (official), local languages
Currency	Franc CFA
Time zone	GMT +0
International phone code	+226
Domain extension	.bf
Main business sectors	cotton, livestock, gold
Main cities	Bobo-Dioulasso, Koudougou
National website	www.primature.gov.bf

Burundi at a glance

Official name	Republic of Burundi *La République du Burundi*
Borders	Democratic Republic of the Congo, Rwanda, Tanzania
Capital	Bujumbura
Population	8.5 million
Official languages	French (official), Swahili, local languages including Kirundi
Currency	Burundi franc
Time zone	GMT +2
International phone code	+257
Domain extension	.bi
Main business sectors	coffee, cotton, hides, sugar, tea
Main cities	Gitega, Muyinga
National website	www.burundi-gov.bi

Cameroon at a glance

Official name	Republic of Cameroon *La République du Cameroun*
Borders	Central African Republic, Chad, Republic of the Congo, Equatorial Guinea, Gabon, Nigeria
Capital	Yaoundé
Population	18.5 million
Official languages	French (official), English (official), Pidgin English, more than 200 local languages
Currency	Franc CFA
Time zone	GMT +1
International phone code	+237
Domain extension	.cm

Main business sectors	aluminium, cocoa, cotton, coffee, crude oil, petroleum products, timber
Main cities	Douala, Garoua
National website	www.spm.gov.cm www.prc.cm

Central African Republic at a glance

Official name	Central African Republic *La République centrafricaine*
Borders	Cameroon, Chad, Democratic Republic of the Congo, Republic of the Congo, Sudan
Capital	Bangui
Population	4.3 million
Official languages	French (official), Sangho, more than 80 local languages
Currency	Franc CFA
Time zone	GMT +1
International phone code	+236
Domain extension	.cf
Main business sectors	agriculture, coffee, cotton, diamonds, timber, tobacco
Main cities	Bimbo
National website	www.diplomatie.gouv.fr/fr/pays-zones-geo_833/centrafrique_354/presentation-republique-centrafricaine_1271/index.html

Chad at a glance

Official name	Republic of Chad *La République du Tchad*
Borders	Cameroon, Central African Republic, Libya, Niger, Nigeria, Sudan
Capital	N'Djamena
Population	10.7 million
Official languages	Arabic (official), French (official), local languages
Currency	Franc CFA
Time zone	GMT +1
International phone code	+235
Domain extension	.td
Main business sectors	cotton, crops, livestock, oil
Main cities	Abéché, Moundou, Sarh
National website	www.primature-tchad.org

Congo at a glance

Official name	Republic of the Congo *La République du Congo*
Borders	Angola, Cameroon, Central African Republic, Democratic Republic of the Congo, Gabon
Capital	Brazzaville
Population	3.7 million
Official languages	French (official), local languages including Lingala, Kikongo, Munukutuba
Currency	Franc CFA
Time zone	GMT +1
International phone code	+242
Domain extension	.cg

Main business sectors	cocoa, coffee, diamonds, natural gas, oil, petroleum, phosphates, sugar, timber
Main cities	Pointe-Noire
National website	www.congo-site.com

Côte d'Ivoire at a glance

Official name	The Republic of Côte d'Ivoire *La République de Côte d'Ivoire*
Borders	Burkina Faso, Ghana, Guinea, Liberia, Mali
Capital	Yamoussoukro
Population	19.2 million
Official languages	French (official), Dioula, Baoule, other local languages
Currency	Franc CFA
Time zone	GMT +0
International phone code	+225
Domain extension	.ci
Main business sectors	bananas, cocoa, coffee, cotton, fish, palm oil, petroleum, pineapples, tropical woods
Main cities	Abidjan, Bouaké, Daloa
National website	www.presidence.ci

Democratic Republic of Congo at a glance

Official name	The Democratic Republic of the Congo *La République démocratique du Congo*
Borders	Angola, Burundi, Central African Republic, Republic of the Congo, Rwanda, Sudan, Tanzania, Uganda, Zambia
Capital	Kinshasa
Population	62.6 million
Official languages	French (official), local languages
Currency	Congolese franc
Time zone	GMT +1 & GMT +2
International phone code	+243
Domain extension	.cd
Main business sectors	cobalt, coffee, copper, diamonds, oil
Main cities	Kananga, Kisangani, Lubumbashi, Mbuji-Mayi
National website	http://www.diplomatie.gouv.fr/fr/conseils-aux-voyageurs_909/pays_12191/congo-republique-democratique_12230/index.html

Djibouti at a glance

Official name	Republic of Djibouti *La République de Djibouti*
Borders	Eritrea, Ethiopia, Somali Republic
Capital	Djibouti
Population	833,000
Official languages	French, (official), Arabic (official), Somali, local languages
Currency	Djiboutian franc
Time zone	GMT +3
International phone code	+253
Domain extension	.dj
Main business sectors	re-exports, hides & skins
Main cities	Dikhil, Tadjoura
National website	www.presidence.dj www.office-tourisme.dj

Gabon at a glance

Official name	Gabonese Republic *La République gabonaise*
Borders	Cameroon, Republic of the Congo, Equatorial Guinea
Capital	Libreville
Population	1.3 million
Official languages	French (official), local languages
Currency	Franc CFA
Time zone	GMT +1
International phone code	+241
Domain extension	.ga
Main business sectors	crude oil, forestry, manganese, mining, petroleum, uranium
Main cities	Franceville, Port-Gentil
National website	www.legabon.org

Guinea at a glance

Official name	Republic of Guinea *La République de Guinée*
Borders	Côte d'Ivoire, Guinea-Bissau, Liberia, Mali, Senegal, Sierra Leone
Capital	Conakry
Population	9.3 million
Official languages	French (official), local languages
Currency	Guinean franc
Time zone	GMT +0
International phone code	+224
Domain extension	.gn
Main business sectors	agricultural products, alumina, bauxite, coffee, diamonds, fish, gold
Main cities	Labé, Kankan, Kindia, Nzérékoré
National website	www.guinee.gov.gn

Haiti at a glance

Official name	Republic of Haiti *La République d'Haiti*
Borders	Dominican Republic, Atlantic Ocean, Caribbean Sea
Capital	Port-au-Prince
Population	9.5 million
Official languages	French (official), Creole (official)
Currency	Gourde
Time zone	GMT -5
International phone code	+509
Domain extension	.ht
Main business sectors	coffee, light manufacturing, mangoes, oils

Main cities	Cap-Haïtien, Carrefour, Delmas, Gonaives, Port-de-Paix
National website	www.haiti.org www.haititourisme.com

Madagascar at a glance

Official name	Republic of Madagascar *La République de Madagascar*
Borders	Island in Indian Ocean off South East Africa
Capital	Antananarivo
Population	19.6 million
Official languages	French (official), Malagasy (official)
Currency	Ariary
Time zone	GMT +3
International phone code	+261
Domain extension	.mg
Main business sectors	cloves, cocoa, coffee, fishing, food & drink processing, forestry, livestock, mining, oil refining, sugar cane, textiles, vanilla
Main cities	Fianarantsoa, Mahajanga, Toamasina
National website	www.madagascar.gov.mg www.madagascar-tourisme.com

Mali at a glance

Official name	Republic of Mali *La République du Mali*
Borders	Algeria, Burkina Faso, Guinea, Côte d'Ivoire, Mauritania, Niger, Senegal
Capital	Bamako
Population	12.3 million
Official languages	French (official), local languages including Bambara
Currency	Franc CFA
Time zone	GMT +0
International phone code	+223
Domain extension	.ml
Main business sectors	cotton, gold, livestock
Main cities	Mopti, Ségou, Sikasso, Tombouctou
National website	www.malitourisme.com

Mauritius at a glance

Official name	Republic of Mauritius *La République de Maurice*
Borders	Island in Indian Ocean (off Madagascar, South East Africa)
Capital	Port Louis
Population	1.2 million
Official languages	English (official), French (official), Creole, Indian languages
Currency	Mauritian rupee
Time zone	GMT +4
International phone code	+230
Domain extension	.mu
Main business sectors	clothing, jewellery, sugar, tea, tourism
Main cities	Curepipe
National website	www.gov.mu www.tourism-mauritius.mu

Niger at a glance

Official name	Republic of Niger *La République du Niger*
Borders	Algeria, Benin, Burkina Faso, Chad, Libya, Mali, Nigeria
Capital	Niamey
Population	14.2 million
Official languages	Arabic (official), French (official), local languages
Currency	Franc CFA
Time zone	GMT +1
International phone code	+227
Domain extension	.ne
Main business sectors	agriculture, gold, livestock, oil, uranium
Main cities	Maradi, Zinder
National website	www.niger-tourisme.com

Rwanda at a glance

Official name	Republic of Rwanda *La République du Rwanda*
Borders	Burundi, Democratic Republic of the Congo, Tanzania, Uganda
Capital	Kigali
Population	9.7 million
Official languages	Kinyarwanda (official), French (official), English (official), Swahili
Currency	Rwandan franc
Time zone	GMT +2
International phone code	+250
Domain extension	.rw
Main business sectors	coffee, hides, tea, tin ore
Main cities	Butare
National website	www.gov.rw; www.rwandatourism.com

Senegal at a glance

Official name	Republic of Senegal *La République du Sénégal*
Borders	Gambia, Guinea, Guinea-Bissau, Mali, Mauritania
Capital	Dakar
Population	12.3 million
Official languages	French (official), local languages
Currency	Franc CFA
Time zone	GMT +0
International phone code	+221
Domain extension	.sn
Main business sectors	cotton, fish, groundnuts, peanuts, petroleum products, phosphates, tourism
Main cities	Thies
National website	www.gouv.sn

Togo at a glance

Official name	Togolese Republic *La République togolaise*
Borders	Benin, Burkina Faso, Ghana
Capital	Lomé
Population	6.5 million
Official languages	French (official), local languages including Kabiye and Ewe
Currency	Franc CFA
Time zone	GMT +0
International phone code	+228
Domain extension	.tg
Main business sectors	cocoa, coffee, cotton, phosphates
Main cities	Sokodé
National website	www.republicoftogo.com

Sources: population data UN (2006) **www.un.org**, local country websites, BBC country profiles, Philips Concise World Atlas.

B: top French companies

This is a list of the largest and most well-known companies in the French-speaking world.

Top companies in Belgium

Company name	Sector
Agfa-Gevaert	digital image products
Almanij	finance
Banque Nationale Belgique	banking
Belgacom	telecommunications
Colruyt	retail
De Post – La Poste	postal services
Delhaize Group	retail
Dexia	banking
Electrabel	utilities
Fortis	finance
Groupe Bruxelles Lambert	industrial
InBev	beverage
Infrabel	railway
KBC Group	finance
Mobistar	telecommunications
SNCB	railway
Solvay Group	pharmaceuticals
UCB	pharmaceuticals

Top companies in Canada

Company name	Sector
Alcan	metal
Bank of Montreal	banking
Bank of Nova Scotia	banking
Bell Canada Enterprises (BCE)	telecommunications
Canadian Imperial Bank of Commerce	banking
Canadian National Railway	railway
EnCana	oil and gas
George Weston	food conglomerate
Husky Energy	energy
Imperial Oil	oil and gas
Magna International	automotive
Manulife Financial	insurance
National Bank of Canada	banking
Nortel Networks	telecommunications

Petro-Canada	oil and gas
Power Corp of Canada	various
Royal Bank of Canada	banking
Sun Life Financial Services	insurance
Toronto-Dominion Bank	banking
TransCanada	utility

Top companies in Luxembourg

Company name	Sector
Arcelor Mittal	steel
CFL	railway
Clearstream	banking
RTL	media
SES Astra	satellite telecommunications

Top companies in France

Company name	Sector
Accor	travel and tourism
Air France-KLM	travel and tourism
AXA Group	insurance
BNP Paribas	banking
Bouygues Group	construction
Carrefour Group	retail
Christian Dior	fashion
CNP Assurances	insurance
Crédit Agricole	banking
Crédit Industriel et Commercial	financial
Crédit Lyonnais Group	banking
Electricité de France	energy and utility
France Télécom	telecommunications
Gaz de France	energy and utility
Groupe Auchan	retail
Groupe Danone	food products
Lafarge	industrial products
L'Oréal Group	personal products

Michelin Group	various
Peugeot Groupe	automotive
Pinault-Printemps-Redoute	retail
Renault Group	automotive
Saint-Gobain	building products
Sanofi-Aventis	pharmaceuticals
SNCF	travel and tourism
Société Générale Group	banking
Suez Group	energy and utility
Total	oil and gas
Veolia Environnement	energy and utility
Vinci Group	construction
Vivendi Universal	media

Top companies in Switzerland

Company name	Sector
ABB Group	electrical equipment
Adecco	commercial services
Baloise Group	finance
Ciba Speciality Chemicals	chemicals
Converium Holding	reinsurance
Crédit Suisse Group	finance
Financière Richemont	luxury products
Holcim	cement
Merck Serono	pharmaceuticals
Nestlé	food products
Novartis Group	pharmaceuticals
Roche Group	pharmaceuticals
Swatch Group	watches
Swiss Life Holding	insurance
Swiss National Bank	banking
Swiss Re Group	reinsurance
Swisscom	telecommunications
Syngenta	agriculture
UBS	financial
Zurich Financial Services	financial

Top companies in French-speaking Africa

Company name	Country	Sector
Sonatrach	Algeria	hydrocarbons
Groupe Ona	Morocco	various
Samir	Morocco	refinery
Office Chérifien des Phosphates	Morocco	mining
Groupe Naftal	Algeria	oil and services
Maroc Télécom	Morocco	telecoms
Société Ivoirienne de Raffinage (SIR)	Côte d'Ivoire	refinery
Algérie Télécom	Algeria	telecoms
Office National de l'Électricité (ONE)	Morocco	energy
Sonelgaz	Algeria	energy
Maroc Phosphore (Groupe OCP)	Morocco	chemicals
NAFTEC	Algeria	refinery
STIR	Tunisia	refinery
Régie des Tabacs	Morocco	agroindustry
Total Gabon	Gabon	hydrocarbons
Orascom Télécom Algérie (OTA)	Algeria	telecoms
Cévital	Algeria	agroindustry
Royal Air Maroc (RAM)	Morocco	transport
Sonara	Cameroon	refinery
Tunisie Télécom	Tunisia	telecoms
Société Nationale des Hydrocarbures	Cameroon	hydrocarbons
Shell Maroc	Morocco	hydrocarbons

Top banks in French-speaking Africa

Company name	Country
Banque Extérieure d'Algérie (BEA)	Algeria
Attijariwafa Bank	Morocco
Groupe Banques Populaires	Morocco
Crédit Populaire du Maroc	Morocco
Banque Nationale d'Algérie (BNA)	Algeria
BMCE Bank	Morocco
Banque de l'Agr. Et du Dév. Rural	Algeria
Banque Centrale Populaire	Morocco
Crédit Populaire d'Algérie	Algeria
Banque Marocaine pour le Com. et l'Ind.	Morocco
Société Générale Marocaine de Banques	Morocco
HSBC Mauritius	Mauritius
Société Tunisienne de Banque (STB)	Tunisia
Banque Nationale Agricole (BNA)	Tunisia
Banque de Développement Local (BDL)	Algeria
The Mauritius Commercial Bank	Mauritius
Banque Internationale Arabe de Tunisie	Tunisia
Crédit du Maroc	Morocco
Banque de l'Habitat de Tunisie	Tunisia
Ecobank Transnational Inc	Togo
Crédit Immobilier et Hôtelier (CIH)	Morocco

Sources: BEL20, CAC40, SBF120, SMI, Forbes 2000 **www.forbes.com**,
Fortune Global 500 **www.money.cnn.com**, The Africa Report Top 500
Companies and Top 200 Banks **www.theafricareport.com**

C: business French template toolkit

A toolkit of templates in French to get you started when doing business in French-speaking countries. Browse each of the models and then mix and match!

Business card/*une carte de visite*

[logo]
[company name]
[company strapline]

Andrea Martins
Directeur marketing

12, rue de la Marquette
75016 Paris Cedex
Tél: 01 00 00 00 00
Fax: 01 00 00 00 01
info@companyabc.fr
www.companyabc.fr

Email/*un courriel*

Madame Carroll,

[text]

Je me tiens à votre disposition pour plus d'information.
Cordialement

Andrea Martins
Directeur marketing

Company ABC

Tél: 01 00 00 00 00
Fax: 01 00 00 00 01
Mobile: 06 00 00 00 00
info@companyabc.fr

www.companyabc.fr
SARL au capital de €50,000

Voicemail messages/*des messages*

Bonjour! Vous êtes sur la messagerie vocale d'Emmanuel Lainé, secrétariat de l'Entreprise ABC. Aujourd'hui le 4 juin, je serais au bureau toute la journée. Cependant, je ne peux répondre à votre appel immédiatement car je suis déjà au téléphone ou sorti pour quelques instants. En cas d'urgence vous pouvez contacter le standard au 01 00 00 00 00 ou me laisser un message détaillé et je vous rappellerai dés que possible. Merci.

Bonjour Mme Carroll, c'est Emmanuel Lainé de l'Entreprise ABC. Nous avons bien reçu les documents et dossiers que nous vous avions demandés lors de notre entretient la semaine dernière.

Cela nous convient parfaitement et nous aimerions vous rencontrer dès que possible pour régler certains détails. Idéalement, jeudi prochain serait le plus convenable. Vous pouvez me contacter tous les jours entre 9 heures et midi au bureau, je vous donne mon numéro de téléphone 01 00 00 00 00. Merci.

Telephone call/*un appel téléphonique*

Personne 1	Personne 2
Allô, bonjour.	Entreprise ABC, j'écoute.
Emmanuel Lainé à l'appareil.	Qui demandez-vous ?
Je voudrais parler à Sarah Carroll.	Vous vous trompez de numéro.
Pourrais-je parler à Mme Carroll ?	Un instant, s'il vous plaît.
Je suis au 01 22 33 44 55.	Ne quittez pas.
Je vous téléphone de la part de Mme Carroll.	Ne coupez pas.
	Il est en ligne.
Je vais patienter.	Sa ligne est occupée.
Puis-je lui laisser un message ?	Je vais voir s'il est là.
	Il est absent aujourd'hui.
Je voudrais laisser un message.	C'est à quel sujet ?
Je rappellerai.	Pouvez-vous attendre ?
	Pouvez-vous rappeler plus tard ?
	Peut-il vous rappeler ?
	Voulez-vous laisser un message ?
	Je lui transmettrai le message.
	Pouvez-vous répéter ?
	Pouvez-vous épeler votre nom?

Letter/*une lettre*

Entreprise ABC   Paris, le 4 juin 2007
12, rue de la Marquette
75016 Paris Cedex
Tél : 01 00 00 00 00
SARL au capital de €100,000

                                        Madame Carroll
                            Cabinet d'Architecte Carroll
                                           06000 Nice

Votre référence : xxx
Notre référence : xxx
Objet : Annonce parue dans « Paris Express »
Pièces jointes : CV

Madame,
A la suite de votre annonce pour un poste de responsable a
l'export…
[text]

[text]
Dans l'attente de votre réponse, je vous prie d'agréer,
Madame, l'expression de mes salutations distinguées.

Cordialement

                                        Andrea Martins
                                   Directeur des ventes
                                             Signature

Advert/*une petite annonce*

cabinet d'architecte
nord de Paris
recherche
secrétaire

Nous sommes une enterprise en expansion ...

Nous recherchons une personne dynamique pour ...

Les candidates devront avoir ...

Anglais indispensable.

Envoyez lettre, CV et photo sous reference 4321 à ...

CV/*un curriculum vitae*

Nom – Prénom 31 ans, célibataire née le 28 septembre 1975	Photo		Adresse: Tél: Mobile: Email:
Ingénieur UTC Compiègne			
Formation			
Cranfield University, UK	Master of Science, Advanced Materials		2000–1
UTC, France	Ingénieur genie méchanique		1997–2000
Lycée	Baccalauréat		1995–7
Expérience professionnelle			
A (nom de la société)	Position. Description des tâches principales. Description des compétences. Expertise particulière.		10/2004– jusqu'à ce jour

| B (nom de la société) | Position. Description des tâches principales. Description des compétences. Expertise particulière. | 12/2002– 09/2004 |
| C (nom de la société) | Position. Description des tâches principales. Description des compétences. Expertise particulière. | 08/2001– 11/2002 |

Langues

Anglais	Courant, diplôme master à Cranfield University
Espagnol	Courant
Allemand	Bon niveau, plusieurs séjours en Allemagne et job d'été (trois mois)

Centres d'intérêts

La pratique régulière de sports: gymnastique, natation, planche à voile
La lecture

Références
1 M. ABC, Entreprise DEF
2 M. GHI, Groupe JKL
3 Professeur MNO, Cranfield University

Balance sheet/*un bilan*

Actif	Passif
actif immobilisé immobilisations incorporelles immobilisations corporelles immobilisations financières	**capitaux propres** capital réserves
actif circulant stocks créances disponibilités	**provision pour risques et** **charges dettes** dettes financiers dettes commerciales fiscals et socials dettes diverses

Organization chart/*un organigramme*

Département	Rôles	Position
Conseil d'administration	Président directeur général (PDG) Vice président Directeur général Conseil de surveillance	
DGA Administration	Secrétariat général Informatique Juridique	Secrétaires Employé(e)s de bureau
DGA Finance	Service de la comptabilité Service des factures Service des statistiques Trésorerie	Chef comptable
DGA Ressources humaines	Service du personnel Relations humaines Organisation Contrat Formation	Chef du personnel

DGA Commercial	Service de publicité Service de promotion Service de marketing Service des ventes Service d'après-vente	Directeur des ventes Chef de publicité Vendeurs
DGA International	Ventes internationales Ventes extérieurs (Union Européene, États-Unis, Moyen Orient, Afrique)	Chef du service des exportations
DGA Production	Service de production Service des achats Service de l'approvisionnement Service des stocks Service de logistique Usine Atelier	Chef de production Ingénieur en chef Responsable des achats Gestionnaire des stocks Chef d'équipe Ouvriers qualifiés Ouvriers specialisés Manoeuvres
DGA R&D	Service recherche Service technique	Directeur technique

D: more information

A summary of all the web links in the culture book, plus some new websites to discover topics related to French business.

You can discover more information about a particular topic or country of interest from the summary of website links that have appeared in this book, but please remember that we have no control over them at all so handle all information with care!

General knowledge

www.academie-francaise.fr
www.alliancefrancaise.org.uk
www.census.gov
www.csa.fr
www.diplomatie.gouv.fr
www.ethnologue.com
www.eu.int
www.euronext.com
www.eurofound.europa.eu
www.francophonie.org
www.g-8.de
www.insee.fr
www.institut-francais.org.uk
www.internetworldstats.com
www.oqlf.gouv.qc.ca
www.un.org

Country knowledge

France

www.acfci.cci.fr
www.afnic.fr
www.ambafrance-uk.org
www.assemblee-nat.fr
www.cnil.fr
www.commerce-exterieur.gouv.fr
www.conseil-constitutionnel.fr
www.conseil-etat.fr
www.culture.gouv.fr
www.diplomatie.gouv.fr
www.douane.gouv.fr
www.elysee.fr
www.entreprises.minefi.gouv.fr
www.impots.gouv.fr
www.industrie.gouv.fr
www.inpi.fr
www.insee.fr
www.justice.gouv.fr

www.legifrance.gouv.fr
www.minefi.gouv.fr
www.minitel.fr
www.nato.int
www.pme.gouv.fr/formations
www.premier-ministre.gouv.fr
www.outre-mer.gouv.fr
www.sarkozy.fr
www.senat.fr
www.sirene.tm.fr
www.un.org
www.wto.org

Belgium

www.belgium.be
www.monarchie.be
www.visitbelgium.be

Luxembourg

www.gouvernement.lu
www.luxembourg.co.uk
www.ont.lu
www.statec.lu
www.visitluxembourg.com

Switzerland

www.myswitzerland.com
www.swissworld.org

Canada

www.canada.gc.ca
www.canada.com
www.chamber.ca
www.statcan.ca

Other countries

Benin **www.benintourisme.com**
Burkina Faso **www.primature.gov.bf**
Burundi **www.burundi-gov.bi**
Cameroon **www.spm.gov.cm**, **www.prc.cm**
Central African Republic
**www.diplomatie.gouv.fr/fr/pays-zones-
geo_833/centrafrique_354/presentation-republique-
centrafricaine_1271/index.html**

Chad **www.primature-tchad.org**
Congo **www.congo-site.com**
Côte d'Ivoire **www.presidence.ci**
Democratic Republic of Congo
http://www.diplomatie.gouv.fr/fr/conseils-aux-
voyageurs_909/pays_12191/congo-republique-
democratique_12230/index.html
Djibouti **www.presidence.dj, www.office-tourisme.dj**
Gabon **www.legabon.org**
Guinea **www.guinee.gov.gn**
Haiti **www.haiti.org, www.haititourisme.com**
Madagascar **www.madagascar.gov.mg, www.madagascar-**
tourisme.com
Mali **www.malitourisme.com**
Mauritius **www.gov.mu, www.tourism-mauritius.mu**
Niger **www.niger-tourisme.com**
Rwanda **www.gov.rw, www.rwandatourism.com**
Senegal **www.gouv.sn**
Togo **www.republicoftogo.com**

Business culture zone

www.chamberonline.co.uk
www.cilt.org.uk
www.metra-martech.com
www.rln-london.com
Maslow hierarchy of needs **www.maslow.com**
Geert Hofstede **www.geert-hofstede.com**
- *Culture's Consequence: Comparing Values, Behaviours, Institutions and Organizations across Nations*
- *Cultures and Organizations: Software of the Mind*
Fons Trompenaars **www.7d-culture.nl**
- *Riding the Waves of Culture: Understanding Cultural Diversity in Business* (with Charles Hampden-Turner)
- *Business Across Cultures* (Culture for Business series) (with Peter Woolliams)
- *Marketing Across Cultures* (Culture for Business series) (with Peter Woolliams)
- *Managing People Across Cultures* (Culture for Business series) (with Charles Hampden-Turner)
- *Managing Change Across Corporate Cultures* (Culture for Business series)

Managing Cultural Differences Lisa Hoecklin
Culture books **www.languageadvantage.com**

Reference zone

Forbes 2000 top companies
www.forbes.com
Fortune Global 500
www.money.cnn.com
The Africa Report – top 500 companies and top 200 banks
www.theafricareport.com

Other useful links

BBC country profiles
http://news.bbc.co.uk/1/hi/country_profiles/default.stm
UK Trade & Investment **www.uktradeinvest.gov.uk**
Management magazine **www.management.fr**
UK Foreign and Commonwealth Office **www.fco.gov.uk**
World Trade Organisation **www.wto.org**
Organisation for Economic Co-operation and Development
www.oecd.org

French media

www.allafrica.com
www.arte.tv
www.canalplus.fr
www.canardenchaine.com
www.europe1.fr
www.france2.fr
www.france3.fr
www.france5.fr
www.humanite.presse.fr
www.la-croix.com
www.la1.be
www.ladeux.be
www.latribune.fr
www.lefigaro.fr
www.lemonde.fr
www.leparisien.fr
www.lesechos.fr
www.liberation.fr
www.m6.fr
www.radio-canada.ca

www.radiofrance.fr
www.rfi.fr
www.rtl.fr
www.rtsr.ch www.tf1.fr
www.tv5.org

French language courses

Teach Yourself French www.teachyourself.co.uk
Michel Thomas French www.michelthomas.co.uk
French language courses www.languageadvantage.com

French dictionaries

Harraps French dictionaires
www.chambersharrap.co.uk/harrap/catalogue/french.php
Académie française dictionary
www.academie-francaise.fr/dictionnaire/index.html
OQLF French dictionary
**www.oqlf.gouv.qc.ca/ressources/bibliotheque/dictionnaires/ind
ex.html**

International business services

Grow Global **www.growglobal.biz**
Optivente **www.optivente.com**

french conversation
jean-claude arragon

- Do you want to talk with confidence?
- Are you looking for basic conversation skills?
- Do you want to understand what people say to you?

French Conversation is a three-hour, all-audio course which you can use at any time, whether you want a quick refresher before a trip or whether you are a complete beginner. The 20 dialogues on CDs 1 and 2 will teach you the French you will need to speak and understand, without getting bogged down with grammar. CD 3, uniquely, teaches skills for listening and understanding. This is the perfect accompaniment to **Beginner's French** and **French** in the **teach yourself** range: www.teachyourself.co.uk.

| teach yourself | **improve your french**
jean-claude arragon |

- Have you got rusty French but don't want to start again?
- Do you want to get up to speed quickly?
- Are you looking for more than the simplest way of expressing yourself?

Improve your French is an ideal way to extend your language skills. You will build on your existing knowledge and improve your spoken and written French so that you can communicate with confidence in a range of situations, and at the same time you will learn about the country and its culture.

| teach yourself | **french** |
| | gaëlle graham |

- Are you looking for an accessible and lively course?
- Do you want to cover the basics then progress fast?
- Do you need to brush up your French?

This brand-new, fully revised and updated edition of the best-selling **French** course will guide you through the basics of the language and provide you with all the tools you need to speak and write confidently. It will offer you lots of opportunities to practise and consolidate your language skills as well as giving you an insight into the culture of the French-speaking world.

french grammar
robin adamson & brigitte edelston

- Are you looking for an accessible guide to French grammar?
- Do you want a book you can use either as a reference or as a course?
- Would you like exercises to reinforce your learning?

French Grammar explains the most important structures in a clear and jargon-free way, with plenty of examples to show how they work in context. Use the book as a comprehensive reference to dip in and out of or work through it to build your knowledge.

teach yourself

From Advanced Sudoku to Zulu, you'll find everything you need in the **teach yourself** range, in books, on CD and on DVD.

Visit **www.teachyourself.co.uk** for more details.

Advanced Sudoku and Kakuro
Afrikaans
Alexander Technique
Algebra
Ancient Greek
Applied Psychology
Arabic
Aromatherapy
Art History
Astrology
Astronomy
AutoCAD 2004
AutoCAD 2007
Ayurveda
Baby Massage and Yoga
Baby Signing
Baby Sleep
Bach Flower Remedies
Backgammon
Ballroom Dancing
Basic Accounting
Basic Computer Skills
Basic Mathematics
Beauty
Beekeeping
Beginner's Arabic Script
Beginner's Chinese Script
Beginner's Dutch
Beginner's French

Beginner's German
Beginner's Greek
Beginner's Greek Script
Beginner's Hindi
Beginner's Italian
Beginner's Japanese
Beginner's Japanese Script
Beginner's Latin
Beginner's Mandarin Chinese
Beginner's Portuguese
Beginner's Russian
Beginner's Russian Script
Beginner's Spanish
Beginner's Turkish
Beginner's Urdu Script
Bengali
Better Bridge
Better Chess
Better Driving
Better Handwriting
Biblical Hebrew
Biology
Birdwatching
Blogging
Body Language
Book Keeping
Brazilian Portuguese
Bridge
British Empire, The

British Monarchy from Henry VIII,
  The
Buddhism
Bulgarian
Business Chinese
Business French
Business Japanese
Business Plans
Business Spanish
Business Studies
Buying a Home in France
Buying a Home in Italy
Buying a Home in Portugal
Buying a Home in Spain
C++
Calculus
Calligraphy
Cantonese
Car Buying and Maintenance
Card Games
Catalan
Chess
Chi Kung
Chinese Medicine
Christianity
Classical Music
Coaching
Cold War, The
Collecting
Computing for the Over 50s
Consulting
Copywriting
Correct English
Counselling
Creative Writing
Cricket
Croatian
Crystal Healing
CVs
Czech
Danish
Decluttering
Desktop Publishing
Detox
Digital Home Movie Making
Digital Photography

Dog Training
Drawing
Dream Interpretation
Dutch
Dutch Conversation
Dutch Dictionary
Dutch Grammar
Eastern Philosophy
Electronics
English as a Foreign Language
English for International Business
English Grammar
English Grammar as a Foreign
  Language
English Vocabulary
Entrepreneurship
Estonian
Ethics
Excel 2003
Feng Shui
Film Making
Film Studies
Finance for Non-Financial
  Managers
Finnish
First World War, The
Fitness
Flash 8
Flash MX
Flexible Working
Flirting
Flower Arranging
Franchising
French
French Conversation
French Dictionary
French Grammar
French Phrasebook
French Starter Kit
French Verbs
French Vocabulary
Freud
Gaelic
Gardening
Genetics
Geology

German
German Conversation
German Grammar
German Phrasebook
German Verbs
German Vocabulary
Globalization
Go
Golf
Good Study Skills
Great Sex
Greek
Greek Conversation
Greek Phrasebook
Growing Your Business
Guitar
Gulf Arabic
Hand Reflexology
Hausa
Herbal Medicine
Hieroglyphics
Hindi
Hindi Conversation
Hinduism
History of Ireland, The
Home PC Maintenance and
   Networking
How to DJ
How to Run a Marathon
How to Win at Casino Games
How to Win at Horse Racing
How to Win at Online Gambling
How to Win at Poker
How to Write a Blockbuster
Human Anatomy & Physiology
Hungarian
Icelandic
Improve Your French
Improve Your German
Improve Your Italian
Improve Your Spanish
Improving Your Employability
Indian Head Massage
Indonesian
Instant French
Instant German

Instant Greek
Instant Italian
Instant Japanese
Instant Portuguese
Instant Russian
Instant Spanish
Internet, The
Irish
Irish Conversation
Irish Grammar
Islam
Italian
Italian Conversation
Italian Grammar
Italian Phrasebook
Italian Starter Kit
Italian Verbs
Italian Vocabulary
Japanese
Japanese Conversation
Java
JavaScript
Jazz
Jewellery Making
Judaism
Jung
Kama Sutra, The
Keeping Aquarium Fish
Keeping Pigs
Keeping Poultry
Keeping a Rabbit
Knitting
Korean
Latin
Latin American Spanish
Latin Dictionary
Latin Grammar
Latvian
Letter Writing Skills
Life at 50: For Men
Life at 50: For Women
Life Coaching
Linguistics
LINUX
Lithuanian
Magic

Mahjong
Malay
Managing Stress
Managing Your Own Career
Mandarin Chinese
Mandarin Chinese Conversation
Marketing
Marx
Massage
Mathematics
Meditation
Middle East Since 1945, The
Modern China
Modern Hebrew
Modern Persian
Mosaics
Music Theory
Mussolini's Italy
Nazi Germany
Negotiating
Nepali
New Testament Greek
NLP
Norwegian
Norwegian Conversation
Old English
One-Day French
One-Day French – the DVD
One-Day German
One-Day Greek
One-Day Italian
One-Day Portuguese
One-Day Spanish
One-Day Spanish – the DVD
Origami
Owning a Cat
Owning a Horse
Panjabi
PC Networking for Small
  Businesses
Personal Safety and Self Defence
Philosophy
Philosophy of Mind
Philosophy of Religion
Photography
Photoshop

PHP with MySQL
Physics
Piano
Pilates
Planning Your Wedding
Polish
Polish Conversation
Politics
Portuguese
Portuguese Conversation
Portuguese Grammar
Portuguese Phrasebook
Postmodernism
Pottery
PowerPoint 2003
PR
Project Management
Psychology
Quick Fix French Grammar
Quick Fix German Grammar
Quick Fix Italian Grammar
Quick Fix Spanish Grammar
Quick Fix: Access 2002
Quick Fix: Excel 2000
Quick Fix: Excel 2002
Quick Fix: HTML
Quick Fix: Windows XP
Quick Fix: Word
Quilting
Recruitment
Reflexology
Reiki
Relaxation
Retaining Staff
Romanian
Running Your Own Business
Russian
Russian Conversation
Russian Grammar
Sage Line 50
Sanskrit
Screenwriting
Second World War, The
Serbian
Setting Up a Small Business
Shorthand Pitman 2000

Sikhism
Singing
Slovene
Small Business Accounting
Small Business Health Check
Songwriting
Spanish
Spanish Conversation
Spanish Dictionary
Spanish Grammar
Spanish Phrasebook
Spanish Starter Kit
Spanish Verbs
Spanish Vocabulary
Speaking On Special Occasions
Speed Reading
Stalin's Russia
Stand Up Comedy
Statistics
Stop Smoking
Sudoku
Swahili
Swahili Dictionary
Swedish
Swedish Conversation
Tagalog
Tai Chi
Tantric Sex
Tap Dancing
Teaching English as a Foreign
    Language
Teams & Team Working
Thai
Theatre
Time Management
Tracing Your Family History
Training
Travel Writing
Trigonometry
Turkish
Turkish Conversation
Twentieth Century USA
Typing
Ukrainian
Understanding Tax for Small
    Businesses
Understanding Terrorism

Urdu
Vietnamese
Visual Basic
Volcanoes
Watercolour Painting
Weight Control through Diet &
    Exercise
Welsh
Welsh Dictionary
Welsh Grammar
Wills & Probate
Windows XP
Wine Tasting
Winning at Job Interviews
Word 2003
World Faiths
Writing Crime Fiction
Writing for Children
Writing for Magazines
Writing a Novel
Writing Poetry
Xhosa
Yiddish
Yoga
Zen
Zulu